LAST LEVEL

Mystery of Sanctification: Book I

(handwritten notes:)
B: — 1
S: —25
C: —14
G: 5.

instagram.
linsedin.
line style.

colour.

by

Shan Lu

(handwritten notes:)
2 S   R 16 1
S 72   G 1 3 3
L 117   B 87

PUBLISHED BY

KRATOS PUBLISHERS

LAST EVE

Copyright © 2020 by Shan Lu

Published by: Kratos Publisher

ISBN: 9798654150813

"I highly recommend this book to you and pray it will change your lives as you read it.

I have personally known Shan Lu for over 10 years and watched her grow into an amazing woman of God. Her insight into the heart of God and desire to help people come into an intimate knowledge of His love and holiness is exceptional. She is a woman of immense integrity and honesty. She loves the Lord with all her heart.

May you be totally blessed as you read this book."

Pastor Ian McCormack
A Glimpse of Eternity Ministry

"The wonderful truth that we are called to pursue a deep relationship with both God and each other is the major heartbeat of the Bible. In her first book Shan has grabbed hold of this and other important themes, she is inviting, or even challenging us to a greater depth of intimacy.

I particularly like the reference to 'spiritual depth' with the Lord and 'spiritual breadth' with our fellow believers.

This book is a diligent and well thought out exposition which draws the reader to a question that must be answered ... can I afford not to be part of the 'profound mystery' that is true intimacy with a living God?"

Pastor Philip Earl
His House

Dedication

To my Lord Jesus, the lover of my soul, for whom I was created and exist, to whom I cling through all seasons of walk, and with whom I am one unto eternity.

To my Dada God, my eternal home, from whom I came, to whom I belong, and in whose arms I am a little child, finding complete love, acceptance and rest.

To my faithful Friend the Holy Spirit, with whom I share the passion to glorify the Son, and who teaches, guides, comforts and strengthens me in this journey.

Acknowledgements

I want to thank and honour my parents, whom God chose before the foundation of the earth to bring me into this world and raise me up. Hoping the best for my life, they sacrificed a lot for me, beside the constant concern for my well-being. I know they will never cease to be a blessing to my life. Mum and Dad, no matter how far I advance in the matters of the kingdom and no matter where I am in the world, I am always your child, and I love you!

I thank the Lord for entrusting me with this assignment, which so far has been the biggest undertaking in my life, and for granting me the grace to complete it, without which it would have been utterly impossible. The process of writing in and of itself has been a journey of growth for me. My prayer is that the Lord will accomplish everything He wants to do through this book (and the rest of the 'Mystery of Sanctification' series that are to come), and that He will receive all the glory!

Contents

I.

Introduction

Where do we begin?

I have many things to say, yet I find it challenging to explain complicated issues in English, which is not my first language, using words that are very limited in and of themselves for communicating spiritual things.

Still my heart so yearns to draw others to my Bridegroom King. It compels me to write that many more may know Him intimately and experience the deep union with Him unceasingly, unbound by the realm of the physical and unhindered by the mundane – such is His desire!

So Lord, help me in my weakness.

Since its founding over 2000 years ago, the representation of the Church on earth has branched into a kaleidoscopic range of various traditions, expressions and practices. In our respective church settings, we can become accustomed to and an expert at running religious programmes, functions and routines, such that we are able to do Christianity on autopilot and do it very well. Nonetheless, one cannot help but ask, "Is there anything more to Christianity than this? If we are really honest with ourselves, are we feeling fulfilled?" Sometimes I wonder, if the Lord Jesus were to tarry indefinitely, would we feel indifferent and simply perpetuate what we do? Also, how much does this type of Christianity appeal to one who is looking from the outside? I suppose I can only speak for myself. As one who is looking from the inside, if this was what Christianity is all about, I would not have considered it worth laying down my everything. For I knew from the beginning that it was a person who found me and has walked with me all these years. It was not a religion or a religious organisation with a set of rules and doctrines that touched the core of my being and changed me forever, but a person – **the Lord Jesus**.

In the centre of Christianity is a relationship – our personal relationship with the living God – not in name only, but to walk with Him daily and remain in constant communion with Him. If we were to sideline such a relationship, immediately Christianity would be reduced to a bunch of religious exercises; dull and shallow. If, God forbid, we were to remove such a relationship, there might not be much left to Christianity. Moreover, among the types of relationships that we have with Christ, we are His disciples, servants, friends, but more than all of these, we are His lovers!

The truth is, Christianity is about a people who, having been redeemed by the precious blood of the Lamb, are being prepared individually and corporately as a Bride for Christ, the Bridegroom King.

Marriage is the ultimate depiction of the kind of relationship that the Lord longs to have with believers; as a husband and wife become one flesh in the marital relationship, He desires to become one with us in the spirit, even as He and the Father are one[1]. The Bible calls this 'a profound mystery'[2].

This aspect of Christianity is not novel. We see in the Old Testament the Lord often relates Himself to His people as a husband to a wife[3]; in the Gospels Jesus is repeatedly likened to a bridegroom[4]; in Ephesians the apostle Paul compares the relationship between Christ and the Church to that of a husband and wife[5]; and in Revelation the apostle John reveals the finale of human history, the culmination of all things, being a glorious Bride made ready for the marriage supper of the Lamb[6].

There has also been a release of the bridal revelation across the body; reflected in the proliferation of bridal-

---

1. (1Co 6:17; Joh 10:30) **2.** (Eph 5:31-32) **3.** (Eze 16; Hos 1-3; Isa 54:5-8) **4.** (Mat 9:14-15; 22:2; 25:1-13; Joh 3:28-29) **5.** (Eph 5:22-32) **6.** (Rev 19:7-9; 21:1-3,9-10)

themed sermons, books and worship songs, we can perceive that more and more believers are being awakened to such a spiritual reality and beginning to pursue personal intimacy with the Lord – much to my joy and excitement!

Nevertheless, from my own experience and observation over the years, it may be said that to many in the body, the Church being the Bride of Christ still remains merely a nice doctrine that makes sense intellectually, yet is irrelevant to everyday living. It may also be said that, among those who have caught the bridal revelation, the understanding of it so far has often been somewhat narrowed to being continually wooed and romanced by the Lord, and its application confined to soaking in His presence, largely separated from the practical life. In addition to the above, having walked through and reflected on some of the painful seasons of testing in my own journey, I came to the realisation that, in order for believers to truly have the freedom to be set apart and prepared as virgins who follow the Lamb wherever He goes[7], there are also some structural and conceptual hurdles that one needs to overcome.

Once a persecuted sect in the Holy Land, today Christians represent roughly one-third of the world's population. Understandably organising such a large body of people is no small task, and institutionalisation would seem an obvious choice for maintaining efficiency, stability and continuity. In modelling after the type of governance commonly seen in the world where a chain of command is usually observed, it naturally follows that believers habitually look to men in ecclesiastical positions for leadership, adhering to their instructions. But we have a dilemma here: no man is perfect or infallible, for it is written, *"All have sinned and fall short of the glory of God"*[8].

Perhaps we can think differently: If Christ to the Church is as a husband to a wife and a head to a body, then as a wife is meant to follow her husband, her head in the marriage, would it not also make sense that all members of the body follow the headship of Christ in our marital covenant with Him[9]? Personally, I am thankful for all the great men and women of God in the body, particularly those from whom I have benefited, and some I am very blessed to call dear friends. Through intimate fellowship, it is interesting to notice that, despite their well-recognised spiritual stature or gifting, they are still humans with weaknesses and struggles and only see in part, just like any of us[10]. This then led me to contemplate the danger and limitation when believers routinely look to the man at the top and devote their lives to serving his vision, which is only part of the jigsaw puzzle. What happened to each member of the body being indispensable and all holding fast to and growing up into Christ the Head, as the Bible teaches[11]? I genuinely believe that our Father in heaven has prepared a wonderful and unique destiny for each of His children, and it is our responsibility to not neglect our own journeys of preparation for such calls, but to fulfil them by following Christ's personal leading step by step through intimacy. Then, instead of uniformity, we will have unity in diversity in the body where each person's maturity is developed, gifting put to use, and destiny fulfilled, according to the manifold grace of God.

An opposite phenomenon which I have come to observe and which sometimes is a reaction against the above, is the independent ambitious pursuit of individual callings at the cost of the corporate good. The truth is, we are unlikely to walk into our own destinies if we only ever operate as lone rangers; rather, as iron sharpens iron[12], we are meant to rub off each other's rough edges, and, in doing so, become part of each other's eternal testimonies of overcoming. Christ is coming back for ONE Bride – a multitude of saints dwelling together in unity[13a].

The mystery of the marriage applies both vertically and horizontally; we are not only to become one with Christ but also one with one another in the Lord; this is what Jesus asked of the Father[13b].

Admittedly the body of Christ is messy, because people are messy; we are all works in progress. In our imperfection, we inevitably hurt one another, and the temptation is to retreat to 'just me and Jesus'. Whilst it is much easier being married to the Lord vertically just as it is much easier being single, there is more glory to be found in being married to the Lord horizontally – the same Lord that dwells in other believers. It takes together *'with all the saints'* to comprehend the *'breadth and length and height and depth'* – all the dimensions of the love of Christ[14]. The marriage, where often two completely opposite individuals become husband and wife learning to love each other selflessly and sacrificing one's own interests and preferences for the sake of the other person, is precisely a picture of how distinct and diverse individuals within the body can become one in Christ. Whereas in the church we often mistake relationships developed through the things shared in common (either spiritual or non-spiritual) for fellowship in the Lord, the reality is that there is no other way to forge true oneness and unity in the spirit other than laying down our lives for one another[15]. That is why the Lord sometimes allows crises to happen so as to refine the 'joints' between different parts of the body[16], in the hope that by our intentionally choosing to obey His commandment to love one another[17], the fellowship among the saints will continually deepen.

I do not claim to know the full answers to the issues highlighted above, for I too see in part and have limitations of my own. Yet my hope is that, by sharing these revelations, I can bring my part, as well as taking others with me on to a journey of intimacy with the Lord, that you too may be smitten with the Bridegroom King and experience the sweet oneness and communion with Him.

Taste and see that the Lord is good[18]!

---

7. (2Co 11:2; Rev 14:4) **8.** (Rom 3:23) **9.** (Eph 5:23-24,28-30; 1Co 11:3) **10.** (1Co 13:9) **11.** (1Co 12:14-27; Col 2:19; Eph 4:15-16) **12.** (Pro 27:17) **13a.** (Psa 133:1) **13b.** (Joh 17:21-22) **14.** (Eph 3:17-19) **15.** (Joh 15:13) **16.** (Eph 4:16; Col 2:19) **17.** (Joh 13:34; 15:12; 1Jn 3:23) **18.** (Psa 34:8)

II.

The Divine Union

Many of us have partaken of the Lord's Supper numerous times in our Christian lives and know that the bread represents the Lord's body that is broken for us and the wine represents the Lord's blood that is shed for us[1]. However, the deeper meaning of the Lord's Supper lies in its allusion to the Jewish betrothal.[2]

In ancient Israel, when a man fell in love with a woman, he would first express his desire to marry this woman to his father, who would then arrange a meeting with the woman's father to discuss such. If her father consented to the marriage and the associated arrangements, the man's father would soon invite the young woman over for an extravagant meal. After the meal, the man would formally present the woman a contract of marriage, called the *ketuba*, along with a bride price, known as the *mohar*. Then he would pour a cup of wine, called the *kiddush cup*. He would first drink half of it, and then pass the remainder to the woman. If she refused to drink from it, it would mean that she rejected the proposal; but if she drank from the same cup, from that moment on she would be officially betrothed to the man. The Jewish betrothal is distinct from the modern engagement as we know, in that it is legally binding. In ancient times, once a betrothal took effect, a man and a woman would immediately be considered husband and wife, although the wedding and consummation would take place later. To cancel a betrothal, it would require a legal divorce. This was the situation with Mary who had been betrothed to Joseph when she was found to be pregnant. The Bible says, *"Before they came together she was found to be with child from the Holy Spirit. And her husband Joseph, being a just man and unwilling to put her to shame, resolved to divorce her quietly."* We know Joseph's plan was stopped by an angel of the Lord[3].

Once the betrothal was concluded, the man and the woman would be separated for roughly a year to prepare themselves for the married life. The man would start building a room for him and his future bride, and usually this room would be adjacent to his father's existing house. Remember, Jesus said, *"In my Father's house are many rooms. If it were not so, would I have told you that I go to prepare a place for you? And if I go and prepare a place for you, I will come again and will take you to Myself, that where I am you may be also"*[4].

Once the room was built, the man would go back for his bride, but when exactly would be determined by his father; the man himself would not know. Again remember, Jesus said, *"Then will appear in heaven the sign of the Son of Man, and then all the tribes of the earth will mourn, and they will see the Son of Man coming on the clouds of heaven with power and great glory… But concerning that day and hour no one knows, not even the angels of heaven, nor the Son,* **but the Father only***… Therefore, stay awake, for you do not know on what day your Lord is coming"*[5]. Also, in another place, He spoke a parable: *"Then the kingdom of heaven will be like ten virgins who took their lamps and went to meet the bridegroom... As the bridegroom was delayed, they all became drowsy and slept. But at midnight there was a cry, 'Here is the bridegroom! Come out to meet him.' ... Watch therefore, for you know neither the day nor the hour"*[6].

So now we understand that when Jesus said, "This cup that is poured out for you is the new covenant in My blood"[7], He was essentially inviting us to enter into a marriage covenant with Him.

After His resurrection, the Lord Jesus ascended to the Father to prepare for us an eternal dwelling place. As Christians, we eagerly await the Lord's return to take us to the marriage supper of the Lamb that we may be with Him forever[8], and that day is drawing nigh...

The theme of marriage ran throughout Jesus' earthly ministry. For example, Jesus spoke to His disciples in parables, saying, *"The kingdom of heaven may be compared to* **a king who gave a wedding feast for his son**"9. When the disciples of John came and asked why they and the Pharisees fasted but His disciples did not fast, Jesus answered, *"Can the wedding guests mourn as long as* **the bridegroom** *is with them? The days will come when* **the bridegroom** *is taken away from them, and then they will fast"*10. John the Baptist also said, *"You yourselves bear me witness, that I said, 'I am not the Christ, but I have been sent before Him.'* **The one who has the bride is the bridegroom**. *The friend of the bridegroom, who stands and hears Him, rejoices greatly at the bridegroom's voice. Therefore this joy of mine is now complete"*11.

The first ever human marriage was created in the Garden of Eden. *The Lord God said, "It is not good that the man should be alone; I will make him a helper fit for him"*12. The Lord God caused a deep sleep to fall upon

1. (Luk 22:19-20) 2. (Mark Davidson. (2010). *Becoming the Beloved*. Shulamite Ministries Publishing. ISBN 9780578048123) 3. (Mat 1:18-21) 4. (Joh 14:2-3) 5. (Mat 24:30,36,42) 6. (Mat 25:1,5-6,13) 7. (Luk 22:20) 8. (Rev 19:7-9) 9. (Mat 22:2) 10. (Mat 9:14-15) 11. (Joh 3:28-29)

the man, and while he slept took one of his ribs and made it into a woman[13]. In parallel, after Jesus was crucified on the Cross, *one of the soldiers pierced His side with a spear, and at once there came out blood and water*[14]. It is by that blood and water believers are justified and sanctified, hence there, out of the side of Christ, the Church was birthed. If Christ is the Last Adam[15], then the Church is the Last Eve. According to His unfathomable wisdom, when God the Father said that it was not good for man to be alone and caused the first Eve to be birthed out of the first Adam's side, He also determined that one day He would cause the Last Eve to be birthed out of the Last Adam's side[16]. Since Woman was taken out of Man, the Bible says that *"a man shall leave his father and his mother and hold fast to his wife, and **they shall become one flesh**"*[17]. Likewise, the Church was taken out of Christ, so she shall leave that which is flesh and blood and be joined to Christ and become one spirit with Him[18]. The apostle Paul called this **'a profound mystery'**[19].

*Wives, submit to your own husbands, as to the Lord. For the husband is head of the wife, as also **Christ is head of the church; and He is the Saviour of the body**. Therefore, just as the church is subject to Christ, so let the wives be to their own husbands in everything. Husbands, love your wives, just as **Christ also loved the church and gave Himself for her, that He might sanctify and cleanse her with the washing of water by the word**, that He might present her to Himself a glorious church, not having spot or wrinkle or any such thing, but **that she should be holy and without blemish**. So husbands ought to love their own wives as their own bodies; he who loves his wife loves himself. For no one ever hated his own flesh, but nourishes and cherishes it, just as the Lord does the church. **For we are members of His body, of His flesh and of His bones.** "For this reason a man shall leave his father and mother and be joined to his wife, and the two shall become one flesh." This is a great mystery, but I speak concerning Christ and the church.*

(Eph 5:22-32, NKJV)

The closest one can be with another person is being one flesh with that person, hence marriage is the most intimate relationship one can have with another human being, and it is a picture of how close the Lord wants to be with His people – as a husband to a wife, becoming one in the spirit.

This heart of the Lord echoes throughout the Bible[20]. In fact, the Bible begins with a marriage, Adam and Eve's marriage, and it closes with a marriage, the marriage of the Lamb and His Bride[21]. Because of the sacred nature of marriage in that it symbolises the union between God and man, the Bible says,

"Let marriage be held in honour among all, and let the marriage bed be undefiled"[22].

Then I saw a new heaven and a new earth, for the first heaven and the first earth had passed away, and the sea was no more. And I saw the holy city, new Jerusalem, coming down out of heaven from God, **prepared as a bride adorned for her husband.** *And I heard a loud voice from the throne saying, "Behold, the dwelling place of God is with man. He will dwell with them, and they will be His people, and God Himself will be with them as their God... Then came one of the seven angels who had the seven bowls full of the seven last plagues and spoke to me, saying, "Come,* **I will show you the Bride, the wife of the Lamb.** *" And he carried me away in the Spirit to a great, high mountain, and showed me the holy city Jerusalem coming down out of heaven from God. (Rev 21:1-3,9-10)*

The Lord spoke through Hosea concerning His people: "*I will* **betroth** *you to Me forever; yes, I will* **betroth** *you to Me in righteousness and in justice, in lovingkindness and in compassion, and I will* **betroth** *you to Me in faithfulness.* **Then you will KNOW** *(Heb: yada)* **the Lord**"[23]. The Hebrew word for 'know' here is **yada**, one of whose applications is for describing intimacy – *"Adam knew (yada) Eve his wife, and she conceived and bore Cain*[24]; *Adam knew (yada) his wife again, and she bore a son and called his name Seth"*[25]. 'Knowing' here literally means **being joined together**, as opposed to merely having certain knowledge about the other person. Therefore 'knowing' the Lord is not just knowing something about Him through the Bible or theological study or spiritual revelation, because knowledge can only take one so far. Paul said, *"We* **know in part** *and we* **prophesy in part... we see in a mirror dimly**"[26]. Merely having knowledge or revelation about the Lord is like seeing in a mirror dimly, as a 'spectator'. One can know every mystery there is to know and still be a 'spectator' until he 'yada' or 'intimately knows' Christ. When we 'yada' Christ, we switch from being 'spectators' to 'participants'. The difference is, for example, you can observe my right arm, you can look at it, touch it, study it, but you will never know it the way I do because it is part of me.

'Intimately knowing' Christ actually means being joined to Christ in the spirit, sharing His very being, and partaking in His divine nature[27].

It was for this kind of 'knowing' that Paul, who was a Pharisee and had much to boast about religious credential and knowledge, wrote, *"I count everything as loss because of the surpassing worth of **KNOWING CHRIST JESUS my Lord.** For His sake I have suffered the loss of all things and count them rubbish, in order that I may **GAIN CHRIST and BE FOUND IN HIM**"*[28]. As to mysteries, God's supreme mystery IS Christ, *in whom are hidden all the treasures of wisdom and knowledge*[29]. When we know Christ intimately, as a husband shares freely with his wife, the Lord naturally shares His heart with us and imparts to us the wisdom of God, which is not like the wisdom of this age or of the rulers of this age[30]. Nevertheless, although **our spirit man becomes one with the Lord upon being born again**[31], he starts off as a baby, and as a baby the level of love one can comprehend and reciprocate is very limited, and, hence, the level of oneness and intimacy one can experience with the Lord is also limited; therefore, what the Lord can share with him is also limited[32]. Only as our spirit man continues to grow through sanctification and as we become more and more 'one' with Him, increasingly the Lord takes us to the greater depths of God[33], and upon reaching entire sanctification, our union with Christ will become complete. Then we shall know the Lord fully just as we also have been fully known[34].

The point is, we do not begin with seeking knowledge or revelation about the kingdom, we seek the person of Lord Jesus; nor do we seek the Lord for knowledge or revelation, we seek Him for Him. For knowledge puffs up[35], whereas knowing the Lord humbles.

---

12. (Gen 2:18) **13.** (Gen 2:21-22) **14.** (Joh 19:34) **15.** (1Co 15:45) **16.** (Gen 2:23; Eph 5:30, NKJV; Rom 5:14) **17.** (Gen 2:24) **18.** (1Co 6:17) **19.** (Eph 5:22-32, NKJV) **20.** (Eze 16; Hos 1-3; Isa 54:5-8) **21.** (Rev 21:1-3,9-10) **22.** (Heb 13:4) **23.** (Hos 2:19-20, NASB) **24.** (Gen 4:1) **25.** (Gen 4:25) **26.** (1Co 13:9,12) **27.** (2Pe 1:4) **28.** (Php 3:8-9) **29.** (Col 2:2-3) **30.** (1Co 2:6-8) **31.** (1Co 6:17) **32.** (Eze 16:3-6) **33.** (Eze 16:7-14; 1Co 2:9-14) **34.** (1Co 13:12)

*Yet **among the mature** we do impart wisdom, although it is not a wisdom of this age or of the rulers of this age, who are doomed to pass away. But we impart a secret and hidden wisdom of God, which God decreed before the ages for our glory ...as it is written,* **"What no eye has seen, nor ear heard, nor the heart of man imagined, what God has prepared for those who love him"— these things God has revealed to us through the Spirit.** *For the Spirit searches everything, even* **the depths of God**... *Now we have received not the spirit of the world, but the Spirit who is from God,* **that we might understand the things freely given us by God**... *The natural person does not accept the things of the Spirit of God, for they are folly to him, and he is not able to understand them because* **they are spiritually discerned.** (1Co 2:6-14)

There were two trees in the midst of the Garden, the tree of life, and the tree of the knowledge of good and evil[36]. Eating of the tree of life speaks of being plugged into God, the Source of Life, as Adam and Eve were before the Fall – they knew God intimately. The moment they disobeyed God and ate of the tree which God had commanded them not to eat, they swapped 'intimately knowing God' for 'knowledge', and from 'participants' they became 'spectators'; they unplugged themselves from the Source of Life, and death came. Since then, the world **has not known** God through its wisdom sprung from the tree of the knowledge of good and evil[37]. But for all Christian believers, Christ became to us wisdom from God[38], **so to advance in true wisdom is to have more and more Christ formed in us through sanctification**[39]. With our willingness and cooperation, the Lord takes us deeper and deeper in sanctification whereby increasingly we become set apart from the world and our mind renewed[40], and, upon completely putting on the mind of Christ[41], we render the tree of the knowledge of good and evil powerless (I will further explain this in another book of the 'Mystery of Sanctification' series). In the end there will only be one tree, the tree of life[42], and to him who overcomes, the Lord will grant to eat of it[43]. Therefore, having eternal life means being plugged into the Source of Life once again as Adam and Eve were at the beginning, that is, becoming 'participants' once again, knowing God intimately and becoming one with Him through Jesus Christ[44], for apart from Him there is no life.

> *And this is eternal life, that they KNOW You, the only true God, and Jesus Christ whom You have sent.* (Joh 17:3)

During His earthly ministry, Jesus taught various parables. Most often, He likened His relationship with His followers to a master with his servants. In John 15:14-15, however, He said, "*You are **My friends** if you do what I command you. No longer do I call you servants, for the servant does not know what his master is doing; but I have called you friends, for all that I have heard from My Father I have made known to you.*" Jesus then, in the parable of the ten virgins, likened Himself to a bridegroom and His followers **virgins who awaited the bridegroom's arrival**[45]. These represent different levels of relationship believers have with Christ: master and servants, friends, **husband and wife**, just like in the temple there are outer court, inner court, the Holy

Place and **the Holy of Holies**, with progressive proximity to God. Song of Songs celebrates the sexual love between Solomon and his bride and is a vivid picture of the spiritual consummation between Christ and His Bride, which is the final result of sanctification. To quote the 1st and 2nd century rabbi Akiva, "All of eternity in its entirety is not as worthy as the day on which Song of Songs was given to Israel, for all the Writings are holy, but Song of Songs is the Holy of Holies."[46] The climax of Song of Songs is Son 8:6-7: *"Set me as a seal upon your heart, as a seal upon your arm, for love is strong as DEATH, JEALOUSY is fierce as the GRAVE. Its flashes are flashes of FIRE, THE VERY FLAME OF THE LORD. Many waters cannot quench love, neither can floods drown it. If a man offered for love all the wealth of his house, he would be utterly despised."*

God is a jealous God[47], and jealousy kills. With this kind of jealousy, Phinehas pierced Zimri and Cozbi with a spear[48], a kind of jealousy a man has for his wife[49], as God warned Abimelech concerning Sarah

Abraham's wife: "If you touch her, you are a dead man"[50].

God is a consuming fire[51], and fire consumes. The closer we wish to draw near to Him, the greater the refinement we have to pass through and the more dross will be burnt up, until there is nothing more to be burnt, by which point we are said to be entirely sanctified.

Being incorporated into the Godhead is being assimilated into His holiness, His divine nature, through burning. As it is written, "You shall be holy, for I am holy"[52]. This is the essence of sanctification. God does not change[53], we have to change. The holy God can only be joined to a holy Bride.

Narrower and narrower is the way. While it is God's desire that all will go all the way to the Holy of Holies by the way Christ opened for us[54], not all will enter; while it is God's desire that all will become the Bride of Christ for there are many rooms in the Father's house, not all will reach the full consummation – **willingness**

on our part to cooperate with God and obey God in the sanctification process being the differentiator. The joy that was set before Christ for which He endured the Cross, despising the shame[55], was not just for winning Himself a bunch of servants or friends, but a Bride. The servants do not know what their master is doing[56]; the friends do not come onto the marriage bed[57]; **only the wife of the Lamb becomes fully one with her Maker Husband[58].** Whilst all the redeemed will dwell in the celestial city of New Jerusalem and will keep developing relationship with God in eternity and eventually come to full maturity, because there is neither time nor negativities as catalysts for sanctification in heaven, for aeons our comprehension of God and the level of intimacy we experience with Him will have been determined by the choices we have made on earth. For our lives on earth will have testified to what proximity we wish to be with the Lord really, and the Lord will respect that, for love does not seek its own[59].

So what about you my friend? Will you make the Lord your only pursuit in this life and pay whatever price it costs to be fully one with Him?

35. (1Co 8:1) **36.** (Gen 2:9) **37.** (1Co 1:21) **38.** (1Co 1:24,30) **39.** (Gal 4:19) **40.** (Rom 12:2; Eph 4:22-24) **41.** (1Co 2:16) **42.** (Rev 22:2) **43.** (Rev 2:7, NASB) **44.** (Joh 17:3,21-23) **45.** (Mat 25:1-13) **46.** (Schiffman, Lawrence H., ed. (1998), Texts and Traditions, Ktav, Hoboken.) **47.** (Deu 4:24) **48.** (Num 25:1-16) **49.** (Num 5:11-31) **50.** (Gen 20:1-7) **51.** (Heb 12:29) **52.** (Lev 11:45; 1Pe 1:15-16) **53.** (Mal 3:6) **54.** (Heb 10:19-22) **55.** (Heb 12:2) **56.** (Joh 15:15) **57.** (Joh 3:29; Heb 13:4) **58.** (Isa 54:5) **59.** (1Co 13:5, NASB)

III.

From Visitation to Habitation

In various places in the Bible, we see occasions where God sovereignly visited man. Some examples are: At Mount Sinai, the Lord invited Moses, Aaron, Nadab, Abihu and the seventy elders of Israel to come up, and they beheld God and ate and drank in His presence. Then the Lord called Moses alone up into the mountain for a more intimate audience with Himself[1]. Twice, the Spirit of God came upon Saul and he prophesied regardless of his own merit (in the second time Saul had turned from the Lord and was pursuing David, but when the Spirit of God came upon him and the two groups of messengers he had sent, they all prophesied[2]). The Lord visited Ezekiel by the Chebar canal. Later, when Ezekiel was sitting in his house with the elders of Judah, the Lord's hand fell upon him and took him by a lock of his hair and brought him in a trance to the temple in Jerusalem[3]. The angel Gabriel was sent from God to Mary to decree the birth of Jesus: *"Behold, you will conceive in your womb and bear a son, and you shall call His name Jesus... The Holy Spirit will come upon you, and the power of the Most High will overshadow you"*[4].

These are all 'VISITATIONS'. In contrast to these occasional encounters, there are other scriptures that describe a rather permanent way of being with God:

One thing have I asked of the Lord, that will I seek after: **that I may dwell in the house of the Lord all the days of my life**, *to gaze upon the beauty of the Lord and to inquire in His temple.*[5]

And behold, the glory of the God of Israel was coming from the east. And the sound of His coming was like the sound of many waters, and the earth shone with his glory... As the glory of the Lord entered the temple by the gate facing east, the Spirit lifted me up and brought me into the inner court; and behold, **the glory of the Lord filled the temple**. *While the man was standing* *beside me, I heard one speaking to me out of the temple, and He said to me, "Son of man, this is the place of My throne and the place of the soles of My feet, **where I will dwell in the midst** of the people of Israel forever."[6]*

*And I heard a loud voice from the throne saying, "Behold, **the dwelling place of God is with man. He will dwell with them**, and they will be His people, and God Himself will be with them as their God."[7]*

***Abide in Me, and I in you.** As the branch cannot bear fruit by itself, unless it abides in the vine, neither can you, unless you **abide in Me**.[8]*

As opposed to 'visitation', these speak about 'HABITATION' – dwelling with God, and abiding in Him.

Through the Pentecostal and the subsequent charismatic movements where the Holy Spirit sovereignly and powerfully manifested, there has been a great spiritual awakening in the body since the beginning of the 20th century. Hearing the older generation and some of my peers who are blessed to have experienced past revivals share how deeply they have been impacted by those outpourings, I am often filled with wonder and gratitude. For, despite not witnessing those events first-hand, like a torch relay, having embraced the fire of God and kept it burning inside, they lit the hunger and passion in me and inspired me to seek God's face from when I was a new-born Christian, which, over time, evolved into a lifestyle. Nevertheless, from my own involvement and from speaking to others in the charismatic circle over the years, I realise that, whereas many are familiar with the occasional 'imposed presence' or 'visitation' of God and would be willing to travel miles to get to a meeting to be touched by the Holy Spirit, not many understand the concept of 'habitation'. But it was 'habitation' that Jesus was referring to when He said, *"In that day you will know that I am in My Father, and **you in Me, and I in You**"*[9], and when He asked of the Father in His high priestly prayer that *"they may all be one, just as You,*

Father, are in Me, and I in You, that they also may be in Us"[10].

The difference is, with 'visitation' we implore and wait for God's presence to come, whilst with 'habitation' we host God's presence and glory by becoming a permanent dwelling place for Him — God's temple, and by permanently abiding in Him[11]. This is a fruit of sanctification.

Since receiving the bridal revelation in the early years of my Christian walk, entering into ever deeper intimacy with the Lord has been my primary pursuit, and it is always a delight to find kindred spirits, the many others who too are smitten with the Bridegroom King. However, in the midst of all the romantic frenzies, I have also observed that some equate intimacy with the Lord to being supernaturally touched by Him. We often hear people talk about 'being blasted by the Spirit', 'being slain in the Spirit' with such great relish as if it is to this end we seek His presence, as if this is the ultimate form of spirituality. A good friend of mine who I hold in high regard and who has ministered in the body around the world for nearly forty years has expressed such a concern, that instead of 'moving towards the Promised Land', some tend to 'camp around the well'. We see in the Bible that the Lord out of His goodness sovereignly provided water for the children of Israel in the wilderness[12]. Yet had the Israelites camped at the waters of Meribah and refused to move on just because they found water, as a people they would have never made it to the promised land.

Whilst the manifest presence of God is wonderful, under which one can be wrapped up in such bliss that the pains and fears of reality dissipate, if care is not taken, the pursuit of God's presence can sometimes turn into a kind of addiction, consumerism or escapism masquerading as spiritual hunger, where the demand for supernatural experiences eclipses the desire for the person of Lord Jesus, all the while resisting God's refinement without which one would not be able to deepen the abiding oneness and intimacy with God, nor walk into his full destiny in God.

When I was a young believer, I too went through a phase of frantically chasing God's presence, attending conference after conference, hoping to receive prophetic words and experience supernatural encounters. Despite the momentary touch of God every now and then, deep down I still felt something was missing, I still felt unfulfilled. Eventually I had to acknowledge that the 'high time' I experienced at those meetings was unsustainable; I would have to keep going to conferences and following those anointed speakers around in order to remain in that place. Looking back, my motive back then frankly was also quite selfish, I was more interested in having my own needs met; I wanted to feel loved, accepted and specially noticed by God; I was pursuing the Lord for me, not Him. This reminds me of the Israelites in the wilderness who grumbled and demanded all the time "Give me bread! Give me water! Give me meat!" and did not care so much about cultivating a relationship with

---

1. (Exo 24:1-2,9-18) 2. (1Sa 10:10-13,19:20-24) 3. (Eze 8:1-3) 4. (Luk 1:26-38) 5. (Ps 27:4) 6. (Eze 43:2-7) 7. (Rev 21:3) 8. (Joh 15:4) 9. (Joh 14:20) 10. (Joh 17:21) 11. (1Co 3:16-17; Col 3:3) 12. (Exo 17:1-7; Num 20:1-13)

the Lord. So, one day, I decided that I would no longer chase the presence, but would simply fellowship with the Lord wherever I am. Before long, it dawned on me that I too have a well in me, and in drinking from that well I have been able to cultivate His presence wherever I am. In fact, those profound encounters I have had with the Lord have often been in the secret place – in my own room with the door closed[13].

In John Chapter 4, pointing at Jacob's well, Jesus said to the Samaritan woman, *"Everyone who drinks of this water will be thirsty again, but whoever drinks of the water that I will give him will never be thirsty again.* **The water that I will give him will become in him a spring of water welling up to eternal life...** *believe Me, the hour is coming when neither on this mountain nor in Jerusalem will you worship the Father... the hour is coming, and is now here, when the true worshipers will worship the Father in spirit and truth, for the Father is seeking such people to worship Him. God is spirit, and those who worship Him must worship in spirit and truth"*[14]. **By the indwelling of the Spirit**[15], Jesus abolished the geographical requirement for worshiping God and its implication for today is such: We do not have to go to a special venue to worship God, nor do we have to shop around for God's presence anymore. Instead, our heart where the Spirit dwells becomes a well[16], our body the living sacrifice, and our life the 24/7 spiritual worship[17]. Rather than looking for water everywhere, we are to learn to dig our own well, just like we cannot always be cheeky and scrounge meals at our neighbours' while never being bothered to cook ourselves, or we may end up becoming the foolish virgins.

The foolish virgins did have the bridal revelation in that they knew they were waiting for a bridegroom, as opposed to a master as depicted in other parables. However, because they were so used to borrowing oil from others, meaning relying on others to bring the manifest presence of God with their anointing instead of being willing to cultivate their own through a lifestyle of love and obedience, which is key to growing in the intimate knowledge of the Lord, in the end they cried,

"Lord, Lord, open to us", but He answered, *"Truly, I say to you, **I do not know you**"*[18].

Symbolism: Oil often represents the anointing of the Holy Spirit, see Luk 4:18, Act 10:38.

Spiritual encounters, though beautiful, are a means to an end. Rather than being only interested in having the Lord continually entertain us, we need to go beyond the momentary encounters. The Lord touches us so that we feel loved enough to embrace the subsequent refinement and pruning, by which we grow in our capacity to be able to host a greater degree of God's presence and glory.

We see in Song of Songs the Lord woos and draws us: *"Arise, my love, my beautiful one and come away… let me see your face, let me hear your voice, for your voice is sweet, and your face is lovely"*[19]. Then immediately after, He says, *"**Catch the foxes** for us, the little foxes that spoil the vineyards, for our vineyards are in* *blossom*"[20]. We are God's vineyard, and catching the foxes speaks of dealing with the sins in our lives that keep us from bearing fruit[21].

As the relationship progresses, the Lord woos us again: *"Behold, you are beautiful, my love, behold, you are beautiful! Your eyes are doves behind your veil..."*[22]. Then straight after in verse 6, He says, *"Until the day breathes and the shadows flee, I will go away to the mountain of **myrrh** and the hill of **frankincense**"*[23]. Now myrrh represents death and suffering while frankincense represents purity and priestly sanctification and intercession. By this point the Lord is saying, "Now you have tasted My goodness[31], but if you want more of Me, you need to follow Me, do as I do, **take up your cross daily and die to yourself** [32], and thus become sanctified as a Melchizedek priest after Me, presenting your body as a living sacrifice, holy and acceptable to God, which is your spiritual worship"[33].

Symbolism: The root of the Hebrew word for 'myrrh' is **marar** [24], meaning 'to be bitter'. It was one of the gifts the Magi brought to the infant Jesus[25], foreshadowing the bitter suffering and death Christ Jesus was to taste for mankind. Myrrh was also used for Jesus' burial[26]. The root word for 'frankincense' in Hebrew is **laban**[27a], meaning 'to be white'. Frankincense was an ingredient of the holy incense burnt on the altar of incense in the desert tabernacle[27b]. When burnt, it emits a white smoke, symbolising pure prayers ascending to God[28]. Like myrrh, it was offered as a gift to the infant Jesus by the Magi[29], signifying His being set apart as the Great High Priest after the order of Melchizedek, holy, innocent and undefiled, to make intercession for us in the true tabernacle in heaven[30].

Then, as the relationship progresses further, the Lord woos us once again: *"You are altogether beautiful, my love; there is no flaw in you"*[34]. But straight after, He says, *"Come with me from Lebanon, my bride; come with me from Lebanon. Depart from the peak of Amana, from the peak of Senir and Hermon, from **the dens of lions**, from **the mountains of leopards**"*[35]. By this stage the Lord is saying, "Since you have been sanctified to a sufficient extent[36], if you will trust Me, come with Me to the battlefields as My warrior bride. In My strength and by My authority you will be able to plunder the enemy's territories"[37].

Symbolism: Wild beasts often represent principalities of darkness over certain spiritual territories. They gain access through the sins of people groups and, in turn, establish demonic strongholds among them[38].

The maidens find it hard to understand the depth of the union between Shulammite and Solomon, because they are only 'onlookers', not 'participants'. They ask, *"What is your beloved more than another beloved, O most beautiful among women? What is your beloved more than another beloved, that you thus adjure us?"*[39a]. Just as the foolish virgins expected to receive the same reward as the wise virgins, the maidens want what Shulammite has yet are unwilling to pay the price. Until the very last minute they are still mere 'onlookers', crying, *"Return, return, Shulammite! Return, return, that we may gaze at you."* But the Lord asks the maidens, *"Why do you desire to gaze at the Shulammite, as at **the**

dance of Mahanaim?"[39b]. Mahanaim is what Jacob named the place where a company of angels met the company of his household[40] – the heavenly coming together with the earthly. Literally translated as 'the dance of two companies', the dance of Mahanaim is said to be a majestic ancient sword dance around a large campfire, an earthly representation of the dance between the Spirit of Jesus and the spirit of the Bride; intertwined, fused, the two become one[41].[42] For when Christ is reproduced and formed in us through sanctification, we will be like Him, reflecting His glory, and will be fully one with Him[43].

To this glorious end, dear friend, will you choose 'habitation' over 'visitation'?

13. (Mat 6:6) **14.** (Joh 4:13-14,21-24) **15.** (Joh 14:17) **16.** (Eph 3:17; Pro 4:23) **17.** (Rom 12:1) **18.** (Mat 25:1-13) **19.** (Son 2:10-14) **20.** (Son 2:15) **21.** (Isa 5:7; Joh 15:1-8; Gal 5:22) **22.** (Son 4:1-5) **23.** (Son 4:6) **24.** (Strong's: H4843) **25.** (Mat 2:11) **26.** (Joh 19:39-40; Heb 2:9) **27a.** (Strong's: H3835) **27b.** (Exo 30:1,6,34-35) **28.** (Rev 8:3-4) **29.** (Mat 2:11) **30.** (Heb 7:11,25-26, NASB; 8:1-2, NASB; Rom 8:34) **31.** (Psa 34:8) **32.** (Luk 9:23) **33.** (1Pe 2:5,9; Rom 12:1) **34.** (Son 4:7) **35.** (Son 4:8) **36.** (Eph 5:25-27) **37.** (Eph 6:10; Mat 28:18) **38.** (Eph 6:12; Lev 26:21-22; 1Co 15:32) **39a.** (Son 5:9) **39b.** (Son 6:13, WEB) **40.** (Gen 32:2) **41.** (Eph 5:21-32) **42.** (Anna Rountree. (2007). *Heaven Awaits the Bride*. pp.241-242. Publisher: Charisma House. ISBN 9781599791746.) **43.** (Gal 4:19; 1Jn 3:2; 2Co 3:18; Rev 21:9-11)

IV.

The Headship of Christ

From my personal journey, I feel one of the keys for continually developing oneness with Christ is understanding and following the headship of Christ.

*For just as the body is one and has **many members**, and all the members of the body, though many, are one body, so it is with Christ... Now you are the body of Christ and **individually members of it**.* (1Co 12:12,27)

*Wives, submit to your own husbands, as to the Lord. For **the husband is the head of the wife even as Christ is the head of the church, His body**, and is Himself its Saviour. Now as **THE CHURCH SUBMITS TO CHRIST**, so also wives should submit in everything to their husbands.* (Eph 5:22-24)

Based on the Scripture, we know it is true that Christ is the head of the church, His body, as the husband is the head of the wife[1], and it is also true that His body is made up of individual members[2]. Then it must be true that Christ is the head of the individual members of His body as the husband is the head of the wife[3]. In this way, a corporate concept is translated into a personal revelation relevant to each and every Christian believer, specifically speaking:

If one knows that Christ is one's personal spiritual husband, then one's walk with Him should be governed by the marriage covenant.

Therefore, will a man tolerate his wife going after another man? Absolutely not! Will a man tolerate another man dictating to his wife? Absolutely not! Then it is unlikely that the Lord will tolerate another man usurping His marital headship over believers, corporately or individually, for He is a jealous God[4]. As Paul wrote,

"I feel a divine jealousy for you, since I betrothed you to one husband, to present you as a pure virgin to Christ"[4a].

Here perhaps we first need to clarify the essence of church. Upon hearing the word 'church', some think of a building with a cross, some think of a religious organisation with a hierarchy of ecclesiastical positions. But what if all the physical church buildings are confiscated or destroyed, does the church still exist? Yes, it does. What if all the institutional church organisations along with their hierarchies collapse, does the church still exist? Yes, it still does. Then what is church? The answer is, it is neither the physical buildings nor the man-made organisations; it is the people, all who believe and are born again in Jesus Christ.

The Church – the 'ecclesia', is comprised of the spirit man of all believers, past, present and future. There is one Church, one body in Christ in the spirit with believers from all geographical locations and all generations[5].

To understand the headship of Christ, we first need to grasp that the church, as opposed to a man-made religious organisation, is a people. For if we consider the church an institutional organisation with a chain of command like those in the secular world where people commonly submit to the dictation of those in senior positions, we would have no problem accepting the headship of man in the church. However, if we consider the church as **a people betrothed to Christ**, then, in the context of marriage, the only person that has the authority to exercise headship is the husband, the head of the marriage, and for each individual believer, Christ is the head in our spiritual marriage to Him.

Whereas the Lord places different types of authority in our life in and outside the church and commands us to submit to them, He has reserved headship to Himself. For headship signifies the final authority in all matters, particularly regarding issues that are directional, whether in the spirit or in the natural, for example, what to believe as truth, or what steps to take in life; and wherever the head leads, the body is supposed to go with it, or we would get a horrific sight, and the oneness a member of the body experiences with the Head would be disrupted. What this means for our practical Christian walk is that, instead of habitually looking to human leaders, as the Bible teaches us, we are to FIX OUR EYES ON JESUS, the author and perfecter of faith[6], and instead of routinely or indiscriminately following the instructions of human leaders, we are to learn to discern and follow the will of God by the inner witness of the Spirit who dwells in each born-again believer[7].

*But I want you to understand that **THE HEAD OF EVERY MAN IS CHRIST**, the head of a wife is her husband, and the head of Christ is God. (1Co 11:3)*

In the Old Testament, the type of government we see among God's people is a corporate structure (or known as the episcopal polity) where one person leads from the top governing through a chain of command. Moses was the first chosen and sent by God to lead the children of Israel out of Egypt after Israel became a people[8]. He functioned as a conduit for the people of Israel, passing on the living oracles received from God to the church in the wilderness[9]. To spread out his burden, he chose able men out of all Israel and made them heads over the people, leaders of thousands, of hundreds, of fifties and of tens; and, later, he gathered seventy men of the elders of Israel to bear the burden of the people with him[10]. Afterwards, Joshua was chosen to succeed Moses to lead the people of Israel into the promised land[11]. After Joshua, intermittently the Lord raised up judges for Israel to alleviate the oppression from the surrounding enemies[12]. Then, in the time of Samuel, the elders of Israel asked for a king to judge them like all the nations. This displeased Samuel, and he prayed to the Lord[13], and the Lord said to Samuel, *"Obey the voice of the people in all that they say to you, for they have not rejected you, but **they have rejected Me from being king over them**. According to all the deeds that they have done, from the day I brought them up out of Egypt even to this day, forsaking Me and serving other gods, so they are also doing to you. Now then, obey their voice; only you shall solemnly warn them and show them the ways of the king who shall reign over them"*[14]. So Samuel warned the people how the king would lord it over them and exploit them[15], but the people insisted, saying, *"No! But there shall be a king over us, that we also may be like all the nations, and that our king may judge us and go out before us and fight our battles"* [16]. Since then, from Saul to David, to Solomon, to the respective successions of kings of the northern and southern kingdoms, to Zerubbabel the governor of Judah, a descendant of David who led the returning exiles to rebuild the temple, Israel always had one man lead from the top. However, the coming of Jesus and the introduction of the New Covenant induced a required shift in the way God's people were to be governed.

Alluding to Jesus, Moses the man of God himself prophesied: **"The Lord your God will raise up for you a prophet like me** *from among you, from your* brothers—**IT IS TO HIM YOU SHALL LISTEN** *...the Lord said to me, '...I will raise up for them a prophet like you from among their brothers.* **And I will put My words in his mouth, and he shall speak to them all that I command him. And whoever will not** *listen to My words that he shall speak in My name, I Myself will require it of him*"[17].

The Lord spoke through Ezekiel: "*I MYSELF WILL BE THE SHEPHERD OF MY SHEEP, and I Myself will make them lie down... And I will set up over them ONE SHEPHERD, My servant David, and he shall feed them: he shall feed them and be their shepherd. And I, the LORD, will be their God, and My servant David shall be prince among them...*"[18].

Finally, Jesus Himself said, "*And I, when I am lifted up from the earth, will DRAW ALL PEOPLE TO MYSELF*"[19].

The first coming of Jesus and the subsequent outpouring of the Holy Spirit at Pentecost fulfilled what God promised through Jeremiah: "*Behold, the days are coming, declares the Lord, when I will make A NEW COVENANT with the house of Israel and the house of Judah, not like the covenant that I made with their fathers on the day when I took them by the hand to bring them out of the land of Egypt,* **My covenant that they broke, though I was their HUSBAND**, *declares the Lord. For this is the covenant that I will make with the house of Israel after those days, declares the Lord:* **I will put My law within them, and I will write it on their HEARTS.** *And I will be their God, and they shall be My people.* **And NO LONGER shall each one teach his neighbour and each his brother, saying, 'Know the Lord,' for THEY SHALL ALL KNOW ME, from the least of them to the greatest**, *declares the Lord. For I will forgive their iniquity, and I will remember their sin no more"*[20].

By the redeeming work of the cross of Jesus Christ and by the indwelling of the Spirit, the way man being with God is reverted to the beginning in the Garden of Eden

1. (Eph 5:23) **2.** (1Co12:12,27) **3.** (1Co 11:3) **4.** (Exo 20:5; 34:14; Deu 4:24) **4a.** (2Co 11:2) **5.** (1Co 12:12-13; Eph 4:4; Rev 2:1,8,12,18; 3:1,7,14; 6:9-11) **6.** (Heb 12:2, NASB) **7.** (Rom 9:1; 12:2; Joh 14:17; 16:13-14; Gal 5:25) **8.** (Exo 1:7; 3:10; Act 7:35-36) **9.** (Act 7:38, KJV; Num 12:2-9) **10.** (Exo 18:21-26, NASB; Num 11:16-17,24-25) **11.** (Num 27:12-23; Deu 1:37-38; 3:23-28) **12.** (Jdg 2:16-19) **13.** (1Sa 8:4-6) **14.** (1Sa 8:7-9) **15.** (1Sa 8:10-18) **16.** (1Sa 8:19-20) **17.** (Deu 18:15-19; Act 3:22-23; Joh 12:47-50) **18.** (Eze 34:11-24; Joh 10:11-16) **19.** (Joh 12:32) **20.** (Jer 31:31-34; Heb 8:8-11) before the Fall – **each having a direct relationship with God, knowing Him intimately, without the necessity for another man to function as an intermediary or a conduit in between**[21]. For under the New Covenant, each born-again believer, whose sin that used to separate him from God has been blotted out by the blood of Jesus, and in whom the Spirit now dwells, has the capacity to be led and taught by God directly, as Jesus quoting Isa 54:13 said, *"They will all be **taught by God**"*[22]; and the Lord promised to guide us into all the truth through the Spirit[23].

Whilst it is biblical and necessary that we have teaching in the church as well as appointing leaders and giving them authority to exercise oversight[24]**, we cannot do so in such a way that infringes on or replaces the headship of Christ, the Husband and Head of individual believers.** Regarding this, the Lord Jesus specifically warned, *"You are not to be called **rabbi**, for you have one **Teacher** (kathégétés), and you are all brothers. And call no man your **father** on earth, for you have one **Father** (patér), who is in heaven.*

*Neither be called **instructors**, for you have one **Instructor** (kathégétés), the Christ. **The greatest among you shall be your servant**"*[25]. Please allow me to elaborate on what this means.

In Jewish education in Jesus' day, from age six Jewish boys would begin 'Bet Safar' to study under the local rabbis. By the end of 'Bet Safar', around age ten, the good ones would have memorised the whole Torah by heart, that is, the first five books of the Bible. From there most boys would go home and become apprentices of family trades such as fishing, farming, carpentry, but the cream of the crop would have the opportunity to progress to 'Bet Talmud'. By the end of 'Bet Talmud', around age fourteen, the good ones would have memorised the entire Hebrew Bible, that is, the entire Old Testament! From there those who did not make the cut would have to go home to learn family business while the best of the best of the best would advance to 'Bet Midrash'. In order to participate in that level of religious education, a boy would have to go and apply to a rabbi and become a disciple of that rabbi who, having interviewed him and recognised his potential, upon admitting him would say, "Come, follow me[26]. Take my yoke upon you and become my disciple"[27]. A 'yoke' is a rabbi's own interpretation of the scriptures and how he has lived it out accordingly, and it varies from rabbi to rabbi. Upon being accepted, that disciple would then devote his entire life to becoming like that rabbi, copying that rabbi, until his teaching, character and way of life were completely reproduced in him[28]. It was in such a context that Jesus said, *"Take My yoke upon you, and learn from Me... My yoke is easy, and My burden is light"*[29].

As believers, it is Christ Jesus THE RABBI that we are called to imitate, and our aim is to have Christ reproduced and formed in us[30], **not another human being.** As the Bible says, *"We are to grow up in every way into Him who is the head, into Christ"*[31].

Meanwhile, the Greek word for 'father' **patér**, according to HELPS Word-studies, means **"one who imparts life** and is committed to it; a progenitor, **bringing into**

being to pass on the potential for likeness". Man was originally made in God's perfect image with a soul bearing the likeness of God[32], but that soul became marred as a result of the Fall[33]. Jesus died on the Cross for all so that by believing and being born-again in Him, man's soul may be restored and enabled to submit to the spirit man who progressively grows into the perfect image of God[34]. As 1Co 15:45-49 says, *"The first man, Adam, became a living* **soul**. *The last Adam became a life-giving* **spirit**... *The first man is from the earth, earthy; the second man is from heaven. As is the earthy, so also are those who are earthy; and as is the heavenly, so also are those who are heavenly.* **Just as we have borne the image of the earthy, we will also bear the image of the heavenly**" (NASB).

It is the image of Christ, who is the image of the Father, that we are to be transformed into[35], **not the image of another 'earthy man'; and it is the heavenly Father alone who is supposed to impart life and likeness to a believer through Christ Jesus.**

When Paul said to the Corinthians, "*I became your father in Christ Jesus*", he was talking about being **an example**, as opposed to a title or superiority or privilege, as seen in the next two verses: "*I urge you, then, be imitators of me. That is why I sent you Timothy… to remind you of my ways in Christ, as I teach them everywhere in every church*"[36]. Paul's '*ways in Christ*' was already stated in the previous paragraph: "*For I think that God has exhibited us apostles as last of all, like men sentenced to death, because we have become a spectacle to the world, to angels, and to men. We are fools for Christ's sake, but you are wise in Christ. We are weak, but you are strong. You are held in honour, but we in disrepute. To the present hour we hunger and thirst, we are poorly dressed and buffeted and homeless, and we labour, working with our own hands. When reviled, we bless; when persecuted, we endure; when slandered, we entreat. We have become, and are still, like the scum of the world, the refuse of all things*"[37]. Paul lived such **a crucified life** that he could boldly say, "If you imitate me, you are effectively imitating Christ[38]. *For I have been crucified with Christ. It is* *no longer I who live, but Christ who lives in me*"[39]. If we are really honest, very few today could make such a claim.

Furthermore, the Greek word used for 'teacher' or 'instructor', **kathégétés**, according to HELPS Word-studies, refers to "a leader; someone bringing others down the road of learning by giving needed instruction; a master-teacher", and according to Strong's Concordance[40], it means 'a guide', suggesting the giving of directional instructions.

Whilst teaching and instructing are needed in the church, as believers we cannot solely rely on or routinely or indiscriminately subscribe to others' teachings without ourselves developing a lifestyle of being led, taught and instructed directly by the Lord through the Spirit, otherwise we risk overriding the headship of Christ with man's.

In the wilderness, God fed the Israelites manna from heaven and permitted each person to gather only as much as he could eat. For beyond such, it could be assumed that one either gathered on someone's behalf or intended to save it for himself for later, and it would breed worms and stink[41]. Bread from heaven usually symbolises the word of God that nourishes our spirit man[42]. It may be said that the purpose for such a 'rationing system' is that, **God wants each person to be fed spiritual food by Him DIRECTLY and DAILY – for it is about relationship – to the amount one can eat and to the level one can digest.** Whilst teachings from others can be beneficial, only the Lord knows fully and exactly where a person is at in his journey, what his spiritual needs are and what he needs to know and do in order to step into the plan He has for him[43]. **At any time, only the Lord is able to provide an instruction precisely tailored to a person; it cannot be substituted by other people's teachings; this is the beauty of walking with the living God who very much cares about and wants to be involved in the details of our life. And following**

Christ's headship means, having discerned correctly and accurately and bearing a clear conscience in the Spirit, following through that specific instruction from the Lord even if or when it is at odds with man's.

Eating manna straight from heaven also has another benefit. We Chinese have sophisticated palates that are very sensitive to variations in the ingredients, because, as a people, we are passionate about quality food and are spoiled by fine cuisine, daily. Similarly, when we become accustomed to the pure manna straight from the throne of God, we develop sensitive **spiritual palates** – the ability to weigh and discern whether a word, doctrine or teaching is from God or not regardless of the stature of the speaker[44]. With such, we are then able to receive others' teachings with discretion, taking a pinch of salt or eating the meat and spitting out the bones if needed. Conversely, habitually feeding on foul food destroys palates. Remember, we are to live by *every word that proceeds out of THE MOUTH OF GOD*[45], be it logos or rhema, not simply out of the mouth of others.

> *But I want you to understand that the head of every man is Christ, the head of a wife is her husband, and the head of Christ is God. Every man who prays or prophesies with his head covered dishonours his head, but every wife who prays or prophesies with her head uncovered dishonours her head, since it is the same as if her head were shaven. For if a wife will not cover her head, then she should cut her hair short. But since it is disgraceful for a wife to cut off her hair or shave her head, let her cover her head... a wife ought to have a symbol of authority on her head... Does not nature itself teach you that... if a woman has long hair, it is her glory? For her hair is given to her for a covering.* (1Co 11:3-15)

Another reason why a man cannot be the head of another is because, exercising headship over someone implies being that person's covering in the context of ownership. Sometimes we confuse covering with accountability. Vertically, eventually we are all accountable to God, while, horizontally, accountability exists between any two believers who have a close relationship and it should work two ways.

Being someone's covering, on the other hand, is assuming total responsibility towards that person's welfare, including protection, provision, upbuilding, etc. in the context of ownership, which is only appropriate and should only exist within the traditional confines of marriage and family.

This is often the case when covering is spoken of in the Bible. When Ruth approached Boaz in the way she did at the threshing floor and said to him, *"Spread the corner of your COVERING over me, for you are my family REDEEMER"*, she was not looking for someone who could give her guidance or someone whom she could be accountable to, but a redeemer to whom she could potentially marry and belong and who would be responsible for her entire provision[46]. Similarly, in Ezekiel when the Lord recounted the things He did for Jerusalem the faithless bride, He said, *"When I passed by you again and saw you, behold, you were at the age* *for love, and **I spread the corner of My garment over you and COVERED your nakedness; I made My vow to you and entered into A COVENANT with you, declares the Lord God, and YOU BECAME MINE***"[47]. Again it is in the context of marriage and headship that 1Co 11:3-15 was written, where Paul insisted that a wife should '**COVER her head**' because she '**ought to have a symbol of authority on her head**', and said that the long hair of a woman '**is given to her for a COVERING**'.

In addition, when children are born from a marriage union, the husband and wife become father and mother, who, in turn, become the co-heads and covering of the children, responsible for their children's welfare. The Bible often mentions *"the heads of the fathers' houses"*[48], and 1Ti 5:14 says, *"I would have younger widows marry, bear children, manage their households"*; the Greek word for 'manage their households' is **oikodespoteó**[49], meaning 'to be the head of a family'.

Therefore, outside the confines of marriage and family, no one is supposed to or able to assume total responsibility towards the welfare of another believer, nor is anyone supposed to own a believer. The role of head and, therefore, covering is reserved for and meant to be fulfilled by Christ Himself, the spiritual head of individual believers, who alone is our Redeemer, Protector, Provider, Author and Perfecter of our faith, and who works 'covering' through the order of marriage and family ordained by God.

As mentioned before, whereas God places different types of authority in our lives and commands us to submit to them, following the headship of Christ means that, in the situations where other types of

21. (Heb 4:16; 10:19-22) **22.** (Joh 6:45) **23.** (Joh 14:17; 16:13-15; Gal 5:18; 1Co 2:12-13) **24.** (Act 2:42; 20:28; Eph 4:11; Rom 12:6-8; 1Ti 3:1) **25.** (Mat 23:8-11) **26.** (Mat 4:19) **27.** (Mat 11:29) **28.** (Rob Bell. *Nooma: 008/Dust*. Produced by Flannel. Published by Zondervan) **29.** (Mat 11:29-30) **30.** (1Co 11:1; Gal 4:9) **31.** (Eph 4:15) **32.** (Gen 1:27; 2:7, KJV; 5:1) **33.** (Rom 3:23) **34.** (2Co 3:18; Col 3:10) **35.** (2Co 4:4; Col 1:15; Joh 14:9) **36.** (1Co 4:14-17; 11:1) **37.** (1Co 4:9-13) **38.** (1Co 11:1) **39.** (Gal 2:20) **40.** (Strong's: G2519) **41.** (Exo 16:14-30) **42.** (Deu 8:3; Mat 4:4) **43.** (Psa 139; Jer 29:11; Pro 16:9) **44.** (Gal 2:6) **45.** (Mat 4:4) **46.** (Rut 3, NLT) **47.** (Eze 16:8) **48.** (1Ch 7:2,7,11,40) **49.** (Strong's: G3616) authority contradict the Lord (provided we have discerned correctly and accurately with a clear conscience), the Lord has to take precedence. However, **there is indeed an exception and a special command from the Lord for wives within marriages**, because in a unique case it overlaps with the headship of Christ[50].

I have explained the unique representation and spiritual significance of marriage, in that it is a picture of the union between Christ and His Bride, and that the Lord is jealous over His people, corporately and individually, and that marriage is to be held in honour among all. It is in such a spiritual context that the Lord commanded, "***Wives, submit to your own husbands, AS TO THE LORD.*** *For the husband is the head of the wife even as Christ is the head of the church, His body, and is Himself its Saviour. Now **AS THE CHURCH SUBMITS TO CHRIST, SO ALSO** wives should submit in everything to their husbands*"[51]. The expressions 'as to the Lord' and 'as the church submits to Christ' convey the significance that for wives, submission to their husbands needs to be of the same importance and degree as their submission to Christ, which ought to be absolute and complete. Furthermore, because the Lord has so designed the government of the institution of marriage as *"the head of every man is Christ, the head of a wife is her husband"*[52], there is, in fact, a chain of command that ought to be observed, namely the order of submission for a wife is first unto the headship of her husband, even if or when she discerns otherwise from the Lord. This is for the wife to remain under her husband's covering and for safeguarding the marriage union between the head and the body[53]; remember, wherever the head leads, the body is supposed to go with it[54]. **The Lord holds the husband accountable for his leadership as the head of the marriage, but He holds the wife accountable for her submission.** This, however, does not condone abuse or domineering, for husbands are also commanded by the Lord to love their wives *"AS CHRIST LOVED THE CHURCH and gave Himself up for her"*[55].

Headship ultimately is designed by God for the purpose of oneness and intimacy, whether it is between a husband and a wife, or between Christ and a believer, or between the Father and the Son, and it is meant to be beautiful and freeing.

Born and bred in a hierarchical society, submission usually is not so much of a problem for me, over-submission is, as those of Asian or African culture might understand. Fortunately, the Lord imparted to me the revelation of His being my Bridegroom at a fairly early stage of my Christian walk and has always drawn me to Himself since, sparing me from chasing Christian ministers or devouring others' teachings, which I imagine could easily have been my trajectory. Nevertheless, that did not fully quench my natural inclination to 'submit' to the great men and women of God, taking seriously and making life decisions based on the things they say. "Whereas Jesus is my lover, in practice I should always listen to my leaders, because they know better and are much more mature and experienced than me", this was how the thinking went.

This went on in the background as I continued growing in my relationship with God, until I hit a season of what I call 'the valley of the shadow of death'... In the midst of pain, scales fell off my eyes, and I realised that church leaders can never be my covering, to look after me, provide for me, to uphold me, comfort me, never hurt me or abandon me, and be fully responsible for the direction they have pointed me to, because, just like me, they are imperfect and have limited power and have their own struggles and weaknesses, and, at times, make mistakes. From speaking to a wise couple who were counselling me through that season, I realised that the Lord at that time was beckoning me to enter into a deeper place of intimacy with Him, and that He would no longer tolerate my looking to another man for headship, because He was very jealous over me, always is, and that the adversities He had allowed me to go through were meant as a wake-up call, in order for me to see that only Christ can be my head. I repented, and I began trying to follow the Lord's direct leading.

The immediate result of such was that, I felt much lighter in the spirit as though an invisible ceiling was lifted off from above my head, and the Lord felt so much closer. I remembered Jesus did say, *"My yoke is easy, and My burden is light"*[56]. Since then, what I have particularly noticed is the coherence of the Lord's leading, which has brought me to walk on a straight path[57], for I became no longer easily tossed to and fro by the waves of men's opinions[58], hence less confusion. Meanwhile, I feel tremendous grace and favour from the Lord in everything He has given me to do, such that working for Him does not feel burdensome, but is full of peace and joy. Moreover, my faith in God has also grown significantly; I have been able to take several leaps of faith including starting to live by faith, knowing that, as long as I obey Him through thick and thin, He will always cover me. Psa 91:14-15 says, *"Because **he holds fast to Me in love**, I will deliver him; I will protect him, because he knows My name. When he calls to Me, I will answer him; I will be with him in trouble; I will rescue him and honour him."* The Hebrew word used for *'hold fast'* here is **chashaq**[59], meaning 'to be attached to; to cling'. I envisage this being as a body attaches itself to the head, following wherever it leads. What this means for me is, I can say to the Lord, "I have followed You and obeyed You scrupulously in everything, I have been careful to remain under Your covering. Now You have to be totally responsible for my welfare." And that is precisely what the Lord has done for me; He has never failed me. This has, in turn, brought an even profounder sense of total belonging and abandonment to the Lord, and enabled me to experience a much deeper level of intimacy and oneness with Him – "*My beloved is mine, and I am His*"[60], and also face up to new seasons of refinement – come what may! There I began to catch a glimpse of the intimacy the Son shares with the Father, His head[61], whom Jesus always followed while walking on earth, as recorded by the apostle John:

*So Jesus said to them, "Truly, truly, I say to you, **the Son can do nothing of His own accord, but only what He sees the Father doing.** For whatever the Father does, that the Son does likewise... I can do* *nothing on My own.* **As I hear, I judge,** *and My judgment is just, because I seek not My own will but the will of Him who sent Me.*"[62]

So Jesus said to them, "When you have lifted up the Son of Man, then you will know that I am He, and that **I do nothing on My own authority, but speak just as the Father taught Me.**"[63]

For I have not spoken on My own authority, but the Father who sent Me has Himself given Me a commandment—what to say and what to speak.[64]

Do you not believe that I am in the Father and the Father is in Me? **The words that I say to you I do not speak on My own authority, but the Father who dwells in Me does His works.**[65]

Jesus demonstrated it for us, so that we who are born again in Him may imitate Him and too walk by the Spirit while on earth, following Christ's personal leading step by step, moment by moment.

Gal 5:25 says, *"If we live by the Spirit, let us also keep in step with the Spirit."* Rom 8:14 says that it is by being led by the Spirit that we are identified as the sons of God. Moses said to the Lord, *"If Your presence does not go with us, do not lead us up from here... Is it not by Your going with us, so that we, I and Your people, may be distinguished from all the other people who are upon the face of the earth?"*[66]. We often say "Emmanuel, God with us", but, in order for God to be with us at all times, we have to follow His leading at all times, just like the Israelites had to follow the pillar of cloud by day and the pillar of fire by night[67]; it does not work the other way round.

In Acts, we see how the early saints tuned in to and were led by the Lord in their coming and going: Philip was led by an angel of the Lord to evangelise to the Ethiopian eunuch and then was translocated by the Spirit of the Lord to Azotus[68]. Ananias, under the direction of the Lord, came to Paul to lay hands on him that he might regain his sight and be filled with the Holy Spirit[69]. Peter, under the guidance of the Spirit, came to Cornelius' house, and the Spirit of God fell on the Gentiles who heard Peter's preaching[70]. Agabus prophesied by the Spirit about the incoming famine which later took place in the days of Claudius, so the disciples were able to send relief to the brothers living in Judea in advance[71]. Peter followed an angel sent by the Lord and walked out of a heavily guarded prison[72]. Under the instruction of the Spirit, Barnabas and Paul were specially set apart for the work amongst the Gentiles[73]. In their subsequent work, they were forbidden by the Spirit to speak the word in Asia, so they went through Phrygia and Galatia. Later, when they attempted to go into Bithynia, they were once again stopped by the Spirit of Jesus[74]. While, at Ephesus, the Spirit pressed Paul to pass through Macedonia and Achaia and go to Jerusalem, and afterwards Rome, and the Spirit testified to him in every city that imprisonment and affliction awaited him[75].

Such a lifestyle is available to every believer according to the grace of God. Empirical evidence shows that it is not limited to the early church, nor to the people adhering to the Pentecostal, charismatic traditions, nor to certain anointed individuals. Jesus is the same yesterday and today and forever[76], and He said,

"My sheep hear My voice, and I know them, and they follow Me"[77].

50. (1Co 11:3) **51.** (Eph 5:22-24) **52.** (1Co 11:3) **53.** (Mat 19:6) **54.** (Eph 5:28) **55.** (Eph 5:25) **56.** (Mat 11:30) **57.** (Pro 3:6; Psa 27:11) **58.** (Eph 4:14) **59.** (Strong's: 2836a) **60.** (Son 2:16) **61.** (1Co 11:3) **62.** (Joh 5:19,30) **63.** (Joh 8:28) **64.** (Joh 12:49) **65.** (Joh 14:10) **66.** (Exo 33:15-16, NASB) **67.** (Exo 13:21; 40:36-37) **68.** (Act 8:26,29,39-40) **69.** (Act 9:10-18) **70.** (Act 10) **71.** (Act 11:27-30) **72.** (Act 12:7-11) **73.** (Act 13:2-4) **74.** (Act 16:6-7) **75.** (Act 19:21; 20:22-23) **76.** (Heb 13:8) **77.** (Joh 10:27)

V.

Submission to Church Authority

I would understand that, for some, the assertion of Christ's headship over individual believers may sound novel and may seem at odds with the traditional understanding of submission to church authority. Here I would like to share my personal revelation on submission to church authority.

In the Greek New Testament, the Greek word commonly used for 'submit' is **hupotassó**[1], including the situations where believers submit to God[2], wives to husbands[3], children to parents[4], citizens to governing authorities[5], bondservants to masters[6], **less mature believers to more mature believers**[7], believers to those devoted to the service of the saints and to every fellow worker and labourer[8], and believers to one another[9].

The Greek word commonly used for 'obey' is **hupakouó**, which, compared with hupotassó, also implies compliance. It is used to express the required obedience from believers to God[10], wives to husbands[11], children to parents[12], bondservant to masters[13], and **believers to spiritual authority**[14].

The most frequently quoted Bible verse for supporting and legitimising the requirement that believers submit to church authority in a legalistic manner is Hebrews 13:17, which commonly translates as *'obey your leaders and submit to them'*. However, the Greek word used here for 'submit' is **hupeikó**[15], a deviation from hupotassó that is used elsewhere to convey the concept of submission, and it occurs only once in the entire Greek New Testament. According to Thayer's Greek Lexicon, hupeikó means **"to resist no longer, but to give way, yield** (properly, of combatants); metaphorically, to **yield to authority and admonition**, to submit". Meanwhile, in the same verse, the Greek word used for 'obey' is **peithó**[16] instead of hupakouó that is used elsewhere to convey the concept of obedience. According to Thayer's Greek Lexicon, peithó means **"to persuade**; (passive) **be persuaded of what is trustworthy"**. Therefore, based on the overall definitions of the two Greek verbs, perhaps Hebrews 13:17 should have been more accurately translated as **'be persuaded by your leaders and yield to them'**, which is more of an exhortation to believers not to be belligerent, unteachable, for those who rule over us watch out for our souls as those who will one day give an account for us before the Lord, as the rest of the verse says[17]. Hence, using Hebrews 13:17 to justify or condone exercising headship or lording it over by church leaders is untenable.

As mentioned in the last chapter, the introduction of the New Covenant brought about a required change in the way God's people were to be governed. As opposed to the kind of governance often seen in the world where one lords it over another through positional authority, under the New Covenant the government of Christ in the kingdom is in the realm of the spirit and is reflected in the natural as a servanthood type of leadership[18].

Jesus said to the disciples, *"You know that the ruler of the Gentiles lord it over them, and their great ones exercise authority over them. IT SHALL NOT BE SO AMONG YOU. But whoever would be great among you must be your SERVANT, and whoever would be first among you must be your slave, even as the Son of Man came not to be served but to serve, and to give His life as a ransom for many"*[19]. Not only so, Jesus Himself demonstrated it by washing the disciples' feet, saying, *"You call me Teacher and Lord, and you are right, for so I am. If I then, your Lord and Teacher, have washed your feet, you also ought to wash one another's feet. For I have given you AN EXAMPLE, that you also should do just as I have done to you. Truly, truly, I say to you, a servant is not greater than his master, nor is a messenger greater than the one who sent him. If you know these things, blessed are you if you do them"*[20].

In a corporate structure (or the episcopal polity), which is the Old Testament model of governance, tacitly the man at the top is the ceiling in terms of spiritual advancement, for, in order to maintain his position and the legitimacy of his leadership, in theory no one is supposed to go above him. In comparison, in a servanthood leadership, bearing great spiritual maturity and authority in the kingdom in the realm of the spirit, one leads BY EXAMPLE and influences from the bottom[21], regardless of whether he holds a position in the natural or not; he willingly functions as a stepping stone or the shoulders others can stand on in order to help others grow in maturity and walk into their destinies in God, desiring to see others exceed him in spiritual advancement.

Besides, in a corporate structure people look up to and rely on the man at the top, and, therefore, place great performance pressure on him who, like any of us, is a mere human, whilst the heart of a servanthood leadership is continually pointing others to the Lord Jesus, instead of drawing others to oneself.

Here we are actually touching on two different types of church authority, POSITIONAL AUTHORITY and

SPIRITUAL AUTHORITY.

Since the inception of the Church, the nature of church authority has undergone significant changes. Christian centres or bishoprics started to form during the Apostolic Age (33-100 AD) with James, the Lord's brother, being the first Bishop of Jerusalem, Peter the first Bishop of Antioch, Paul and Peter the first joint Bishop of Rome, and Mark the Evangelist the first Bishop of Alexandria. Moreover, before the issuance of the Edict of Milan by Constantine and Licinius in 313, in the first 300 years the church faced great persecutions from Jews, pagans and, most of all, the totalitarian Roman state, from confiscation of property to exile, to imprisonment, to execution, by sword, griddle, pyre and wild beasts... countless Christians suffered gruesome tortures and met the end of martyrdom, men and women alike, young and old alike. In the same period, the church also had to fight rampant heresies within and paganism, Greek philosophies, without. Amidst such a hostile environment and turbulent time, apostolic succession was, thus, implemented to ensure that orthodox doctrines could be passed down to posterity.

Also, the Lord raised spiritual leadership to be a stabilising force in the church to bring wisdom and strength to believers, men who lived righteous and holy lives, who were heresy-detesting, uncompromising and vigilant, and who were prepared to be martyred for Christ at any time. Over time, these men's spiritual authority was recognised by those around them, and they rose to ecclesiastical positions such as bishops.

By the time Christianity was accepted by the Roman Empire, the church had been more or less purged of false believers, false doctrines, and its canon confirmed, creed formed, theology developed – it was time to spread and expand!

Riding on the official sanction and the power and resources granted by the state, I can imagine that, with her new-found freedom and favour, the church was only too eager, too ambitious to firm her footing and establish her presence within the Empire, earnestly seeking to maximise the spreading of the Christian faith. Such excitement arguably might have overshadowed and, therefore, caused the church to overlook some of the side effects of the marrying of the church and the state that she later was proved to be less prepared for, among which were the interference of the state in ecclesiastical affairs, replacing personal conviction and devotion to Christ with legalistic organised religion enforced by both church authority and the state, and complacency and corruption creeping into the clergy on account of power and prestige. Yet, despite these, the church managed to navigate through the ebb and flow of history over the next 1200 years. By God's grace and her stewardship, Christianity grew from a persecuted sect originated from the Holy Land to an established religion over the whole Europe, commanding respect and submission from even the heads of the nations. Nevertheless, the outstanding issues such as those mentioned above increasingly took a toll on the church, and eventually culminated in the advent of the Protestant Reformation in the early 16th century.[22] In particular, it may be said that one of the key underlying causes was that some of the ecclesiastical officials inherited the positions along with their associated powers, yet failed to live up to the standards of virtue of their predecessors, the aforesaid spiritual leadership in the early church who emerged out of the persecution fire.

Essentially, there occurred a separation and, thus, a differentiation between positional authority and spiritual authority in the church, leading to sometimes a mismatch between the two, which arguably can still be observed in the present day.

When speaking about church authority, usually it is positional authority that people are referring to, as it is the more recognisable of the two. An ecclesiastical position inherently has authority attached to it, and that authority is granted by the religious organisation it belongs to – an institution set up by man; and its level of authority depends on where in the hierarchy of the organisation man places it.

This means, the authority of an ecclesiastical position cannot be exercised outside the jurisdiction of the religious organisation where the position lies. Meanwhile, positional authority is fully transferable, in that whoever succeeds a position also succeeds its attached authority regardless of the person's own virtues. In other words, positional authority lies with the position, not the person who fills the position.

The implication of such is that, for example, prior to the Reformation, some of the clerics in the church

1. (Strong's: G5293) **2.** (Eph 5:24; Heb 12:9; Jam 4:7) **3.** (Eph 5:24; Col 3:18; Tit 2:5; 1Pe 3:1,5) **4.** (Luk 2:51) **5.** (Rom 13:1,5; Tit 3:1; 1Pe 2:13) **6.** (Tit 2:9; 1Pe 2:18) **7.** (1Pe 5:5) **8.** (1Co 16:15-16) **9.** (Eph 5:21) **10.** (Heb 5:9; 11:8) **11.** (1Pe 3:6) **12.** (Eph 6:1; Col 3:20) **13.** (Eph 6:5; Col 3:22) **14.** (Php 2:12; 2Th 3:14) **15.** (Strong's: G5226) **16.** (Strong's: G3982) **17.** (NKJV) **18.** (Joh 18:36) **19.** (Mat 20:25-28; 23:11; Luk 22:25-26) **20.** (Joh 13:3-17) **21.** (2Th 3:9, NKJV) **22.** (Eusebius of Caesarea (263-339AD). *The History of the Church.* (1989). Publisher: Penguin Classics. ISBN 9780140445350) (Earle E. Cairns. (1996). *Christianity Through the Centuries: A History of the Christian Church.* Publisher: Zondervan. ISBN 9780310208129) **23.** (Earle E. Cairns. (1996). *Christianity Through the Centuries: A History of the Christian Church.* Publisher: Zondervan. ISBN 9780310208129) conducted their lives just like those in the world, yet they could still exercise positional authority over believers.[23]

Spiritual authority, on the other hand, lies with the person who may or may not hold an ecclesiastical position in the natural. Part of the spiritual authority a person carries is warranted by the extent and the depth of sanctification he has undergone and the spiritual battles he has fought and won, and part of it is determined by what the Lord sovereignly bestows on him for the work of ministry.

This means, the specific areas in which one has spiritual authority and the degree to which they do, are spiritually objective; they are not subject to man's interpretation, nor manipulation. In addition to the aforementioned early church leaders who endured severe persecution fire, the apostle Paul, for instance, also carried great spiritual authority. For as to sanctification, he lived a totally crucified life[24]; as to spiritual battles, he fought against beasts[25], that is, principalities; and as to sovereignly delegated authority, he was entrusted with special authority by the Lord for his ministry which has been impacting the church even to this day. While warning those unrepentant among the Corinthian church who doubted his authority[26], he wrote, *"For this reason I write these things while I am away from you, that when I come I may not have to be severe in my use of the authority that the Lord has given me for building up and not for tearing down"*[27]. Unlike positional authority, spiritual authority can be exercised anywhere the Lord sends the person, and its transferability is conditional on that person being received. If we recognise the spiritual authority a person carries and receive and honour that person, we would then be able to glean from that person and, therefore, grow in the same areas of influence that person operates in[28]. As Jesus said, *"The one who receives a prophet because he is a prophet will receive a prophet's reward, and the one who receives a righteous person because he is a righteous person will receive a righteous person's reward"*[29].

As to those leaders in the early church, it may be said that they first had a significant amount of spiritual authority on account of their righteous walk and severe refinement, as well as the sovereign conferment of the Lord, and then they correspondingly had positional authority added in the natural as they stepped into ecclesiastical positions. However, as their bishoprics were passed down as part of the church tradition, from reading church history, it seems the vital importance of spiritual authority gradually became overlooked in the church, such that positional authority simply became synonymous with church authority.

Before heeding the call of the Lord to serve Him full-time, as part of my professional career, I worked in human resource management at the headquarters of a Chinese commercial bank, specifically in head counting and recruiting. Due to such experience, I often draw a parallel between the 'church authority conundrum' above and a work challenge that I used to face back there.

Revolving around the design and improvement of the organisational structure and positions of our firm, there was a constant debate between **the position-orientated approach** and **the person-orientated approach**: Do we create a position first based on business and organisational analysis and then recruit the person who best fits the role, or do we bring on a competent talent first and then create a position for him? Our HR division favoured the former, because, from the back office's perspective, it was more systematic, methodological and more necessary for oversight to keep the firm's overall human resource cost under control, whereas the business divisions favoured the latter, because from the front office's perspective it was more practical, flexible and more able to accommodate immediate business needs. During those years, I was often caught in heated debates, even head-to-head confrontations with various representatives from the business divisions, not only needing the grace and boldness from the Lord, but also sometimes finding myself desperately trying to borrow that extra oomph from my three-inch heels!

Working for the Human Resource Department, I had an obligation to stand by the HR policy of the firm, but I was also required to empathise with our counterparts who contended for extra human resources which they often believed to be the key missing ingredient in order for their parts of the business to succeed. Subject to the stance and approval of senior management, at times I had to dig my heels in and contest their requests, because oftentimes they were so preoccupied with the interests of their own divisions that they overlooked the overall interests of the firm. At other times, it was necessary to yield to them because their divisions had genuine needs, and meeting those needs would benefit the business as a whole, for I understood that the organisational structure, along with its positions, needed to have the flexibility to adapt to the ever-changing business environment. From doing some research and speaking to others in the HR industry, I found out that which approach is favoured really varies from corporation to corporation, depending on the nature of the business, the company culture and the management preference, etc. But when it comes to the kingdom, I think we need both!

We cannot build the house of the Lord haphazardly, solely being driven by individuals' callings or particular passions towards certain aspects of the Christian ministry; we need a structure and different offices and functions therein[30] – the position-orientated approach (I will further explain this in another book of the 'Mystery of Sanctification' series). In the meantime, because the church is the people, needless to say our arms are always wide open to anyone who wishes to join God's household; and as believers grow, mature through discipleship, their gifting and calling will gradually make room for them and define their individual roles and functions in the church – the person-orientated approach. The fundamental key is, we need to allow the Holy Spirit to direct us and help us organise the church in the natural based on THE SPIRITUAL REALITY, that is, determining and maintaining ecclesiastical positions and appointing people to those positions according to what the Spirit shows us, in terms of whom, where they are at maturity wise, what offices or/and giftings they have, how they function in the spirit, etc.[31], so that those wielding positional authority in the natural are the same people carrying corresponding levels of spiritual authority in the realm of the spirit like in the early church, or at least there is a strong positive correlation between the two. Conversely, organising ecclesiastical positions in the church based on human wisdom according to how things appear in the natural is likely to result in a mismatch of reality of what is in the spirit and what is in the natural.

Furthermore, having fallen short of the glory of God[32], we humans have an ever-present need to maintain a sense of security and, therefore, tend to stick to what we know – conventions, and, over time, we have developed a dogmatic tendency. Yet the revelation of Jesus is always expanding, the Holy Spirit is always moving; the spiritual realm is very dynamic[33]! Rather than clinging onto human rules and traditions, the church can only rely on the Lord's leading for its continual survival and 'thrival'. What has always been is not always true, what has worked in the past does not necessarily work every time[34], and what has arisen to serve a specific purpose at a specific time does not warrant perennial existence. The Lord does not only have 'entry strategies' but also 'exit strategies', meaning a ministry or a ministerial position sometimes is not meant to last forever. For no matter how valid, how legitimate at the time it came, once it has accomplished its kingdom purpose, it is time for it to exit and its people disbanded who may be regrouped later for other assignments of God. The body of Christ needs to be mobile, flexible and attentive to the Lord's leading at all times.

Whereas positional authority is obvious, it is not as easy to recognise spiritual authority since it is in the realm of the unseen[35], yet we have not been left without a clue. This takes us back to the issue we were discussing earlier – church governance, more specifically, the Old Testament model versus the New Testament model of governance. As shared previously, the Old Testament model is one man governing at the top through a chain of command – this is effectively achieved through the exercising of various levels of positional authority within a religious organisation, whilst the New Testament model is a servanthood type of leadership – leading, serving and influencing others from the bottom.

In a servanthood leadership, often the greater one's kingdom stature in the spirit the lowlier one appears in the natural[36].

For example, in terms of the order of importance of functions in the body, the Bible says that *"God has appointed in the church first apostles, second prophets"*[37], but when it comes to spiritual stamina, the Bibles says that the house of the Lord is *"built on the foundation of the apostles and prophets, Christ Jesus himself being the cornerstone"*[38], meaning that, although those genuinely walking in these two offices carry great spiritual authority and maturity, they position themselves at the lowest, together with the

Lord Jesus who *"came not to be served but to serve"*[39] holding the weight of the house of God at the bottom. The apostle Paul is an example. Though being a spiritual giant in the kingdom, he said that he was *"the very least of all the saints"*[40a] and that God had exhibited him along with other apostles as *"last of all"*[40b]. Pouring out his heart before the Corinthians, he wrote, **"What we are is known to God, and I hope it is known also to your conscience"** – in terms of spiritual stature in the realm of the unseen – *"We are not commending ourselves to you again but giving you cause to boast about us, so that you may be able to answer those who boast about* **outward appearance** *and not about what is in the heart"*[41a]. Highlighting the contrast between what appears in the natural and what actually is in the spirit, he continued, *"We are treated as impostors, and yet are true;* **as unknown, and yet well known**; *as dying, and behold, we live; as punished, and yet not killed; as sorrowful, yet always rejoicing;* **as poor, yet making many rich; as having nothing, yet possessing everything"**[41b].

It can be said that recognising spiritual authority was a journey of learning for Nicodemus, who himself as a Pharisee, ruler of the Jews and teacher of Israel held positional authority[42]. He recognised that God was with Jesus, so he humbled himself and came to Him by night, and Jesus taught him the difference between that which is of the flesh in the natural and that which is of the Spirit[43]. Later, when his fellow Pharisees sought to arrest Jesus because He was drawing people away and were afraid that those of the authorities and of the Pharisees had also believed in Him, Nicodemus spoke up in Jesus' favour despite facing hostility from His colleagues[44]. It is not unreasonable to assume that there, Nicodemus saw the difference between someone who tried to exercise power and control through positional authority and someone who walked in great spiritual authority yet in **love and humility**. In the end, while the disciples had fled and Peter denied the Lord three times[45], it was Joseph of Arimathea, a member of the Sanhedrin (another with positional authority), who came to Pilate asking for Jesus' crucified body. Nicodemus also came with spices, and together they buried Him[46]. It may be inferred that, by then, Nicodemus had recognised who Jesus really was in the spirit and willingly submitted to His authority. Concerning the centurion who firmly believed in Jesus' spiritual authority (Jesus never held positional authority), Jesus *marvelled and said to those who followed Him, "Truly, I tell you, with no one in Israel have I found such faith"*[47].

Having distinguished and discerned between positional authority and spiritual authority in our church life, we can then submit more 'accurately', neither subjecting ourselves to false yokes, nor failing to submit to church authority[48].

Without undermining Christ's headship, with positional authority we honour and submit to them in the Lord, for ultimately *there is no authority except from God*[49]. With those carrying great spiritual authority, not only do we honour and submit to them, but sometimes it is also necessary that we receive them with *'fear and trembling'*, because they are ambassadors for Christ, speaking and working under the direction and on the authority of the Lord[50], and their words and works impact us significantly[51], whether in the spirit or later manifesting in the natural, whether individually or corporately.

Whilst in any circumstances we do not want to come under the control of man simply on account of their positional authority, we also need to **be careful not to go into independence or rebellion**, which is easy to do under the influence of the spirit of the world[52], especially for those who have been hurt or abused by those in ecclesiastical positions in the past. While we all hope that the representation of the Church on earth is a holy place of ethereal perfection and beauty, until she is fully sanctified, unfortunately we come across sad stories that we ourselves sometimes are part of. It always grieves me whenever I see on the news or hear from fellow Christians about the injustice individuals have suffered to various degrees at the hands of church leaders. Without condoning it, I am, on the other hand also concerned about the aftermath of such, which I have sometimes observed among believers, and that is,

in the absence of walking through forgiveness and healing, the trauma from the past can cause a victim to be repelled by the notion of submission to church authority of any sort.

This can be further exacerbated by the prevalent worldly ethos of 'equality', which believers in the West in general are more exposed to, and which, if care is not taken, can lure us into discarding and, therefore, disobeying God's commandment regarding submission to authority altogether.

In the kingdom, whilst we are all 'equal' in that we are all unconditionally loved and accepted by God in Jesus Christ and that He has assigned a calling and destiny to each of us[53], we are NOT all 'equal' in the extent to which we have been through the sanctification process and grown in maturity and authority and walked into our callings and destinies; these are affected by the degrees of our willingness to cooperate with God and the choices we make in our Christian walks; NEITHER are the sizes of our callings or levels of spiritual authority sovereignly given by the Lord all 'equal'; the Bible says that there are *"leaders of thousands and of hundreds, of fifties and of tens"*[54], and that some are entrusted with five talents, some with two and some with one[55].

If we are of dust and clay, then God is the Master Potter[56], and in pottery it takes processes such as grinding, moulding, trimming, drying, glazing and, most importantly, rounds of intense firing in order for a vessel to become beautiful, presentable and ready for use. As individual believers, we are at different stages of preparation for the different purposes we are designed for, be it being trimmed off of excessive pride, or left in the wilderness to dry, or glazed with new gifting, or put through the fire of testing...[57] In 2Ti 2:20-21, Paul wrote, *"In a great house there are not only vessels of gold and silver, but also of wood and clay,* **some for honour and some for dishonour.**

Therefore IF ANYONE CLEANSES HIMSELF from the latter, he will be A VESSEL FOR HONOUR, SANCTIFIED and useful for the Master, prepared for every good work"(NKJV). This means a part of the spiritual authority that can be grown into for the works of the kingdom is conditional on ourselves as believers, i.e. our resolve to continually pursue righteousness and holiness and persevere in the spiritual battles ordained for us. Meanwhile, to demonstrate God's sovereign choice, Paul also wrote in Rom 9:20-21, *"But who are you, O man, to answer back to God? Will what is moulded say to its moulder, 'Why have you made me like this?' Has the potter no right over the clay, to make out of the same lump one vessel for honourable use and another for dishonourable use?"* Now this is the part of the spiritual authority that is *not because of works but because of Him who calls*[58].

So in the spirit there is indeed a hierarchy of maturity and authority, and we are exhorted by the Word of God to submit to those more mature than us and obey those with great spiritual authority[59].

Nevertheless, even one with great spiritual authority cannot infringe on Christ's headship over another believer for the reasons I have already explained in the last chapter.

24. (Gal 2:20) 25. (1Co 15:32) 26. (2Co 13:3) 27. (2Co 13:10) 28. (2Co 10:13) 29. (Mat 10:41) 30. (Eph 4:11; Rom 12:4; 1Co 12:18) 31. (Act 20:28) 32. (Rom 3:23) 33. (Joh 5:17) 34. (2Sa 5:17-25) 35. (2Co 4:18) 36. (Mat 11:29) 37. (1Co 12:27-28) 38. (Eph 2:20) 39. (Mat 20:28) 40a. (Eph 3:8) 40b. (1Co 4:9) 41a. (2Co 5:11-12) 41b. (2Co 6:8-10) 42. (Joh 3:1,9) 43. (Joh 3:2,6) 44. (Joh 7:45-52) 45. (Mat 26:31-34,56,69-75) 46. (Mar 15:43; Joh 19:38-40) 47. (Mat 8:5-13) 48. (Mat 11:29-30; 23:2-4) 49. (Rom 13:1) 50. (2Co 5:20; 7:15) 51. (Mat 10:1,5,14-15,40; Luk 10:1,16) 52. (1Co 2:12; Eph 2:1-3) 53. (Rom 2:11) 54. (Exo 18:25, NASB; Deu 1:15, NASB) 55. (Mat 25:14-30; Luk 12:48) 56. (1Co 15:48; 2Co 4:7; Isa 64:8) 57. (Jill Austin. (2003). *Master Potter*. Destiny Image Publishers. ISBN 9780768421729) (Jill Austin. (2005). *Master Potter and the Mountain of Fire*. Destiny Image Publishers. ISBN 9780768421903) 58. (Rom 9:11) 59. (1Pe 5:5; Php 2:12; 2Th 3:14)

VI.

Fellowship in The Lord

In order for marriage to be called 'a profound mystery' of the church, there is still one more significant aspect yet to be discussed, and that is, we are not only to become one with Christ, but also one with one another in the Lord; the mystery of the marriage applies both vertically and horizontally. This is what Jesus asked of the Father in His high priestly prayer: *"That they may all be ONE, just as You, Father, are in Me, and I in You, that they also may be in Us... The glory that You have given Me I have given to them, that they may be ONE even as We are ONE, I in them and You in Me, that they may become perfectly ONE..."*[1].

Adding to the various historical schisms and divisions, there has been a proliferation of individual ministries and parachurch organisations, leading to further fragmentation of the representation of the body of Christ on earth[2].

In a universal sense, the bond believers have with one another in Christ cannot be broken, because, in the vertical dimension, individually we are one spirit with Christ[3], the Head, who holds the members of the body together[4]. However, if we are to speak from experience, perhaps many would say that, in the horizontal dimension, the degree of oneness shared among believers has been somewhat short of the fullness.

From what I can see, with what we are given and what we know, we try our best to do the corporate life together, often uniting ourselves under, firstly, on the spiritual front, common religious tradition, theology, gifting, calling, ministry, worship and so on, and secondly, on the non-spiritual front, common locality, culture, skin colour, social class, wealth status, talent, standpoint, etc. But, admittedly, in the status quo most of us probably cannot, with a clear conscience, make such a statement, that the quality of relationships with Christians is always better than that with non-Christians. Besides, sometimes we witness or ourselves experience the frailty of fellowships when conflicts arise and seemingly strong relationships break apart.

The Lord with His wisdom is able to use all the relationships in the church for good, even those that are largely worldly, fleshly[5], but the truth is, for deep, satisfying and lasting fellowships that will continue onto eternity, we will need to shift the basis of how we relate to one another from the natural to the spiritual and from 'outside' Christ to 'IN' Christ, for it is 'IN' Christ that believers truly become ONE.

It can be argued that the items on the two lists above under which believers unite can all exist independently outside or **without** Christ. The second list is out of the question, but even the items on the first list, though appearing spiritual and having merit in themselves, do not always have to be 'in' Christ. As to religious tradition, we know the Jews had been observing the religious tradition based on the Mosaic Law given by the Lord Jesus in the wilderness in His pre-incarnate state[6], yet when He Himself came in their midst, they could not recognise Him[7]. As to theologies, we know there are scholars who know the Bible inside out and are experts in theologies, yet they do not believe in Jesus[8]. As to gifts and calling, we know they are irrevocable[9], which means if a person falls from grace, he can nonetheless continue exercising his gifts. As to ministries including worship bands, we know they can be financially self-sustaining through product or ticket sales like any secular business independent of the Lord.

Therefore, even when the things believers unite under are supposedly spiritual, they do not always guarantee that the relationships are 'IN' Christ.

I think one of the key causes of the oneness among believers being suboptimal is that we often mistake UNIFORMITY for UNITY.

For just as the body is one and has many members, and all the members of the body, though many, are one body, so it is with Christ. For in one Spirit we were all baptised INTO ONE BODY—Jews or Greeks, slaves or free—and all were made to drink of one Spirit. (1Co 12:12-13)

True unity is found 'IN' Christ and in it there should be diversity, i.e. distinct individuals united as one in Christ while retaining their respective qualities. Gal 3:27-28 says, *"For as many of you as were baptised into Christ have put on CHRIST. THERE is neither Jew nor Greek, THERE is neither slave nor free, THERE is no male and female, for you are all ONE IN CHRIST JESUS."* We do not cease to be Chinese, Asians, Africans, Europeans... just because we become one. True unity embraces different races, skin colours, cultures, nationalities, stations, sexes, ages, personalities, giftings, callings... without elevating one group of people above others or favouring one over others, and then expecting the rest to align. On the contrary, as seen in Isaiah 60, varieties of 'wealth' from the nations, which represent the sons and daughters of God from all corners of the earth with their respective spiritual heritages and treasures, are needed for beautifying the house of the Lord and making it glorious[10].

Uniformity, on the other hand, is based on commonality; it is essentially human allegiance formed according to the things people share in common, spiritual or non-spiritual, with a tacit 'membership condition' that if anyone wants to be a part, he has to conform to the group, become like those in the group.

Uniformity, therefore, tends to lead to the kind of problem described in 1Co 12:14-19: a single member purporting to be the whole body, be it an eye, an ear, a hand or a foot, the partial claiming to be the whole, considering and presenting itself as all there is about Christianity. Although uniformity can temporarily project a picture of 'unity' locally, in the grand scheme of things it actually leads to persisting divisions in the body, for we end up with various sizes of clusters of believers that fellowship based on the things shared in common which are not necessarily 'in' Christ, and that have limited fellowship with other believers who do not conform to their commonality.

If we are to move from uniformity to true unity, the below medley of scriptures may shed some light:

*"We know that **our old self was crucified** with Him*[11]*. From now on, therefore, we **regard no one according to the flesh**... **if anyone is IN Christ, he is a new creation**[12]. He Himself is our peace, who has **made us both one** and has **broken down in His flesh the dividing wall of hostility**... that He might **create IN HIMSELF ONE NEW MAN in place of the two**, so making peace, and might reconcile us both to God **in ONE BODY** through the cross, thereby **killing the hostility**[13]. ...seeing that you have **put off the old self** with its practices and have **put on THE NEW SELF**, which is being renewed in knowledge after the image of*

*its Creator. **HERE there is not Greek and Jew, circumcised and uncircumcised, barbarian, Scythian, slave, free; but CHRIST IS ALL, AND IN ALL**[14]".*

The 'HERE' in the last sentence refers to our spirit man or **the Christ formed in us**[15], **THE NEW SELF** that is being renewed after the image of Christ through crucifying the old, in reference to the previous sentence. In other words, the new self is the key for uniting diverse individuals within the body in Christ. It may be said that the main reason why, so far, we have experienced limited oneness in the body is because, often the way we relate to one another is more according to the flesh forming human allegiance between the old selves than according to the Spirit being united in the one new man in Christ through crucifying the old selves. Human allegiance is feeble, divisible; only Christ cannot be divided[16]. Deep, meaningful and everlasting fellowships are a result of sanctification, i.e. putting off the old self, which belongs to the former manner of life and is corrupt through deceitful desires, and putting on the new self, created after the likeness of God in true righteousness and holiness[17]. For it is the same Christ formed in you and formed in me that writes off our differences according to the flesh and that is respectively joined to the Lord who, in turn, makes us one 'IN' Himself. As to human allegiance, even though temporarily it gives an impression of 'unity', compared to the true oneness in the Lord resulting from the horizontal outworking of the mystery of the marriage, it is more like 'cohabitation'.

The story of the Tower of Babel in the Bible is an example of 'cohabitation'[18]. The motive for building the Tower of Babel was 'becoming a community' and 'becoming famous'. The children of man were united as 'one people' behind such pursuits and had 'one language' among themselves. But the Lord came down and deliberately caused confusion and misunderstanding among them. So, in the end, they had to abandon what they had set out to do and each went his own way.

> *And they said to one another, "Come, let us make bricks, and burn them thoroughly." And* **they had brick for stone, and bitumen for mortar**. *Then they said, "Come, let us build ourselves a city and a tower with its top in the heavens, and* **let us make a name for ourselves, lest we be dispersed over the face of the whole earth**." *And the Lord came down to see the city and the tower, which the children of man had built. And the Lord said,* **"Behold, they are ONE PEOPLE, and they have all ONE LANGUAGE,** *and this is only the beginning of what they will do. And nothing that they propose to do will now be impossible for them. Come,* **let Us go down and there confuse their language, so that they may not understand one another's speech." So the Lord dispersed them from there over the face of all the earth**, *and they left off building the city.* (Gen 11:3-8)

The obvious reason for which the Lord's hand was against the building of the Tower of Babel was that the project was for self-glorification as opposed to glorifying God; the children of man wanted to make a name for themselves by building something high and lofty for all to see. The Word says, *"**God opposes the proud** but gives grace to the humble"*[19]. Another less mentioned yet very important reason was that, the kind of 'oneness' they had was illegitimate.

There is a grand vision in the heart of God for mankind: the children of man are to become one 'IN' the Son and through the Son become one with the Father[20].

Though having great potential to accomplish mighty things, the type of 'oneness' those building the Tower of Babel had was 'outside' the Son and was human allegiance in nature, founded on the common interests of making a name for themselves and avoiding being dispersed over the face of the whole earth. This was also reflected in their choice of materials for building the Tower of Babel; they had 'brick' for 'stone', and 'bitumen' for 'mortar'.

Stones, being natural material, symbolise the works of the Spirit, untainted by fleshly effort. We see in the Bible that structures pertaining to God or the kingdom are often made of stones unspoiled by the flesh, such as the altar the Israelites built to the Lord[21], Solomon's temple[22], and the stone that represented the kingdom of God that struck the image of iron, clay, bronze, silver and gold and became a great mountain filling the whole earth in Nebuchadnezzar's dream[23]. In contrast, bricks, such as those building the Tower of Babel made, symbolise fleshly means. Similarly, mortar, which consists of natural materials, signifies the bond formed 'in' Christ in the spirit, whereas bitumen, which melts in heat, speaks of human allegiance 'outside' Christ that often falls apart amidst the fire of testing.

The spiritual house of the Lord can only be built with what saints are in the spirit as 'LIVING STONES' forged through living the crucified life, not with what we do according to the flesh, and the living stones have to be joined together with 'mortar' – being bonded in the spirit 'IN' Christ the one new man by putting to death our old selves[24]. Only in this way can God dwell among us who are His temple[25], that He may be in us and us in Him, fulfilling the grand vision in the heart of God for mankind. For God does not dwell in a house made by human hands[26]. (I will expound on the mystery of the building in another book of the 'Mystery of Sanctification' series.)

Lastly, another reason why the Tower of Babel was denied longevity was because it was a self-sustaining project founded on human co-dependence without any need to depend on God. The Word says, *"All flesh is like grass and all its glory like the flower of grass. The grass withers, and the flower falls"*[27]. In order for any of our works to have lasting impact and eternal significance,

1. (Joh 17:21-22) **2.** (Earle E. Cairns. (1996). *Christianity Through the Centuries: A History of the Christian Church*. Publisher: Zondervan. ISBN 9780310208129) **3.** (1Co 6:17) **4.** (Eph 4:15-16) **5.** (Rom 8:28) **6.** (Jud 1:4-5) **7.** (Joh 8:19) **8.** (Joh 5:39-40) **9.** (Rom 11:29) **10.** (Hag 2:7-9; Isa 60:11; Rev 21:24-26) **11.** (Rom 6:6) **12.** (2Co 5:16-17) **13.** (Eph 2:14-16) **14.** (Col 3:9-11) **15.** (Gal 4:19; Col 1:27) **16.** (1Co 1:13) **17.** (Eph 4:22,24) **18.** (Gen 11:1-9) **19.** (Jam 4:6) **20.** (Joh 17:21-22) **21.** (Deu 27:5-6; Jos 8:31) **22.** (1Ki 6:7, NASB) **23.** (Dan 2:34-35,44-45) **24.** (1Pe 2:5; Eph 2:20-22) **25.** (1Co 3:16; Rev 21:3) **26.** (Act 7:48; 17:24) it has to be done according to the will of God and carried out by His grace. This means, discern what God wants us to do and how to do it and when[28], and do it with the strength, gifts, platforms, resources, etc. provided by Him, such that we have nothing to boast but give all glory to God.

The failing of the Tower of Babel and the scattering of those building it confirm what Jesus said: "***Whoever is not with Me is against Me, and whoever does not GATHER WITH ME scatters***"[29].

The above has an implication for the Christian corporate life, that is, whenever we gather together as a community or on account of a shared Christian cause, if our motive is for making a name for ourselves, if the basis on which we associate with one another is a common benefit or pursuit as opposed to being joined together 'IN' Christ through living the crucified life, or if we count on a self-sustaining system built with worldly wisdom or resources from man for continuity, then it is possible that the Lord's hand may hinder it;

and even if it appears successful and spiritual and the people are united behind it, it nonetheless has the risk of being a 'Tower of Babel'. The Lord may still use it for good for a period of time[30], but, eventually, He will bring it through the fire of testing to reveal what sort of work it is[31]; to what extent the fruit of its works and the relationships formed in the midst will abide[32].

"Do not think that I have come to bring peace to the earth. I have not come to bring peace, but a sword. For I have come to set a man against his father, and a daughter against her mother, and a daughter-in-law against her mother-in-law. And a person's enemies will be those of his own household. Whoever loves father or mother more than Me is not worthy of Me, and whoever loves son or daughter more than Me is not worthy of Me. And whoever does not take his cross and follow Me is not worthy of Me. Whoever finds his life will lose it, and whoever loses his life for My sake will find it."* (Mat 10:34-39)*

In Mat 10:34-39, Jesus said that He did not come to bring peace, but a sword, and then He listed the closest human relationships on earth on which He was about to wield the sword. Jesus was not saying that it was permissible to dishonour father or mother, for, on other occasions, He confirmed God's commandment about honouring father and mother[33].

Rather, what He meant by bringing a sword was that, God refines human relationships, and it often involves breaking human allegiance, human co-dependence.

In some cultures, allegiance or commitment to another human being, be it a family member, friend, employer or leader, is extolled as the highest virtue or presented as an obligation, and nonconformists are chastised. Yet the Lord is saying, "Watch, how I break the false allegiance, break off the false yoke!" And He does so by allowing an adverse situation to come up to serve as a catalyst to expose the selfish motives of the hearts and the corrupt nature of the flesh. Usually when a person's interests are threatened or when a person is driven to desperation, what he is really made of would be exposed.

Peter thought he would be willing to go with Jesus both to prison and to death, but when danger came, he denied the Lord three times just as the Lord had foretold[34]. When Samaria was besieged by the army of Syria, there was a great famine; mothers against their nature resorted to cannibalism devouring their own children, as Moses had prophetically warned Israel against forsaking the Lord some 600 years before[35]. The same thing happened again during the siege of Jerusalem by Titus, the son and successor of the Roman Emperor Vespasian (69-79 AD), about 40 years after Christ's ascension, according to the Jewish historian Josephus (37-100 AD).[36] Because *all have sinned and fall short of the glory of God*[37], unless born again in Jesus Christ and subsequently progressively renewed through sanctification, man has a propensity for selfishness at the cost of others. Whilst such hides well behind the façades in normal times, it will usually be exposed under the pressure of conflicts. That is why when many believed in Jesus on account of the signs He was doing, *Jesus on His part did not entrust Himself to them, because He knew all people,* **He knew what was in man**[38]. Regarding our pathetic selfish fallen nature, Winston Churchill was spot on: "We have no lasting friends, no lasting enemies, only lasting interests." Therefore, oftentimes, human allegiance is effectively using each other, and it only takes the removal of the 'uniting interest' for human allegiance to break, and a 'uniting interest' can be material, psychological, or even spiritual.

The breaking up of human allegiance, despite its well-intended end, which I will explain shortly, is nonetheless painful, as any who has been through such would concur. At times, it would seem as if the entire relationship is jeopardised because of the overwhelming feeling of hurt and disappointment.

The truth is, a relationship between two believers is typically a mixture of fellowship in the Lord and human allegiance, and it is only the latter that is tested. Whenever this happens, we always have a choice.

Without going through forgiveness and healing, some unfortunately become so disheartened that they choose to retreat from the corporate Christian life into independence and isolation, settling for 'just me and Jesus', or keeping others at an arm's length to prevent themselves from getting hurt again. However, if knowing the Lord intimately is, as shared before, being joined to the Lord in the spirit, sharing **His very being**, then the Christian life can never be 'just me and Jesus', because **the body of Christ** encompasses many believers. Whereas our personal intimate walk with the Lord gives us spiritual 'depth', our walk with other members of the body in the Lord gives us spiritual 'breadth', without which our knowledge of Christ would be limited and incomplete. As it is written in Eph 3:17-19, *"So that Christ may dwell in your hearts through faith—that you, being rooted and grounded in love, may have strength to comprehend WITH ALL THE SAINTS* *what is the breadth and length and height and depth, and to know the love of Christ that surpasses knowledge, that you may be filled with ALL THE FULLNESS OF GOD"*, it takes together *'with all the saints'* to comprehend the *'breadth and length and height and depth'* – all the dimensions of the love of Christ.

An often overlooked way of furthering our personal oneness and intimacy with the Lord is through the horizontal dimension.

Whilst it is much easier being married to the Lord vertically just as it is much easier being single, there is more glory to be found in being married to the Lord horizontally – the same Lord that dwells in other believers. Individually, we are fashioned differently and have unique life journeys and walks with the Lord with distinct callings and destinies[39]. Since each of us is most aware of our own journey and the set of understanding of God derived therein, the temptation is that we extrapolate our own to others, assuming ours is the conclusive and inclusive truth about Christianity. However, what each of us represents and brings to the body, no matter how profound it may be, is only one of the many facets about Christ; individually we all know in part[40], whether one is a famous preacher or a nameless nobody.

By journeying with others, recognising, witnessing and, by God's leading, participating in the works of the Lord in others' lives, our horizon can be widened, that we may learn the manifold wisdom and grace of God in His redemptive work among men and thus comprehend even more the vastness of His love.

Therefore, the Christian life has to be not only 'individual' but also 'corporate'. That is why Heb 10:25 exhorts us: *"Not giving up meeting together, as some are in the habit of doing"* (NIV).

As shared earlier, the corporate life is not meant to be at the cost of individuality (in terms of uniformity), but, at the same time, **neither should the personal**

spiritual pursuit be at the cost of the corporate life. Our personal devotion to the Lord, if it has true depth, will naturally extend and overflow to the Lord's heart's desire, which is the justification, sanctification and fulfilment of destiny of each human being on earth, such that the Lord's passion becomes our passion, and we are willing to do anything and allow ourselves to be used in whatever way to facilitate that. In my own horizontal walk, in awe I have discovered that, working towards the total restoration of mankind, the Lord faithfully journeys with every individual and is willing to work around all kinds of human sins and weaknesses, wrong motives and choices, and causes all things to work together for good[41], in order to put each person in the best position to accomplish as much as possible that which has eternal significance within his lifetime, with such patience, such love. For me, as it is written, *"Such knowledge is too wonderful for me; it is high; I cannot attain it"*[42]. Being very aware of my own weaknesses, I feel utterly humbled and challenged.

In the process of learning horizontal relationships, at times I cannot help but moan that it is so much easier and simpler to just fellowship with the Lord! The Lord is perfect and He always works around my needs, but people are complicated; they have all sorts of motives and opinions and are often self-centred; they have free will that even God will not override and that is not always exercised to one's own best interest in terms of spiritual advancement. In my vertical relationship with God, usually I only need to pay attention to two things, one, is my heart right, and two, have I heard the Lord correctly and accurately. However, journeying in the horizontal dimension, so many more concerns have been added, such as where is the person at in his maturity, which area of his life is God currently working on, have I myself overcome in that area, do I have enough relationship with the person to speak into that area, have I been given the authority to do so, have those events designed to prepare his heart for receiving the word taken place, to what degree will he receive the word and actually act on it? I have lost count of how many times I misjudged and messed up. To be honest, sometimes it can be tiring and frustrating. But I know it is the Lord's will that I persevere in the horizontal relationships and keep serving others. For He showed me that the Father serves all His children selflessly and tirelessly to raise us up, having to work around our needs and will, and, in doing so, imparts His life to us; I ought to be like my Father to serve like a mother, working around her little ones' needs and will, without expecting anything in return[43] – my reward is with Him in eternity. **This really requires me to take focus away from myself and learn to become more selfless.** For love does not seek its own, but bears all things, believes all things, hopes all things, endures all things[44]. Such was Paul's heart when he wrote: *"For though I am free from all, I have made myself **a servant to all**, that I might win more of them. To the Jews I became as a Jew, in order to win Jews. To those under the law I became as one under the law (though not being myself under the law) that I might win those under the law. To those outside the law I became as one outside the law (not being outside the law of God but under the law of Christ) that I might win those outside the law. To* *the weak I became weak, that I might win the weak.* **I have become all things to all people, that by all means I might save some. I do it all for the sake of the gospel, that I may share with them in its blessings**"[45].

The horizontal journey is in essence A JOURNEY OF SELFLESSNESS. Our God is totally selfless, we see such selflessness demonstrated by each member of the Trinity: The Holy Spirit loves the Son and glorifies the Son; He works in and through all things and all men, yet remains invisible that the Son may get all the glory. The Son loves the Father and glorifies the Father; He **EMPTIED HIMSELF** by taking the form of a servant and obeyed the Father to the point of death, that the will of the Father might be done[46]. The Father loves us; He did not withhold His only begotten son, but gave Him as a ransom for mankind, that all the children of man might be reconciled to Him and become one with Him through the Son and partake in the oneness of the Trinity.

Therefore, as opposed to holding onto offence, judging others and shying away from the corporate Christian life, while facing the break-up of human allegiance, we have another choice: forgive and be healed and learn to become more selfless in our horizontal relationships. As we become more selfless, we grow to be more like the Lord, that is, more Christ is formed in us. Then, individually, we become more one with the Lord, and, corporately, more one with one another in the Lord. Such is the horizontal application of the mystery of the marriage, and such serves to forge true oneness in the body.

Jesus prophesied that the great tribulation in the last days would be so severe that *"many will fall away and betray one another, brother will deliver brother over to death, and the father his child, and children will rise against parents and have them put to death"*[47].

This is a sharp contrast with His commands to us that we are to love one another and lay our lives down for one another[48]. Perhaps all human allegiances will fall apart under the extreme pressure of the end-time tribulation; only deep fellowships formed in the Lord will have the stamina to stand such severe fire of testing.

The true depth and strength of a fellowship may be illustrated in this way: Say how much Christ is formed in a person is from a scale of 0 to 10. If person A has 3 and person B has 5, then 3 is the real depth of their fellowship in Christ. Say person C has 8, then, between B and C, the depth of their fellowship would be 5, whilst between A and C it would still be 3. As you can see, the true depth of a fellowship between two believers is the overlap of the 'Christ formed within' and is constrained by whoever has less. This is because TRUE SPIRITUALITY boils down to how much Christ is formed in a person, rather than the level of gifting or calling, or the extent of theological knowledge or spiritual revelation, or the outward success of one's ministry[49]; and TRUE FELLOWSHIP is the 'Christ formed in you' and the 'Christ formed in me' being joined 'IN' the Lord in the spirit. For this reason, the Lord continually refines the relationships between believers, so that by dismantling the human allegiance part of our relationships, we may focus on growing and deepening the true fellowships in Him – by our intentionally preferring others over ourselves in selfless love – this is what laying our lives down for one another essentially means. In other words, the refinement of relationship is part of the normal Christian life, the key is how we respond, i.e. whether we choose to obey the Lord's command to love one another.

The marriage, where often two completely opposite individuals become husband and wife learning to love each other selflessly and sacrificing one's own interests and preferences for the sake of the other person, is a picture of how distinct and diverse individuals within the body can become one 'in' Christ, unto eternity, which ecumenism at a diplomatic level would never be able to achieve. The mystery of the marriage is the 'superglue' that brings about the indestructible eternal oneness with God and with one another, which temporal human allegiance founded on commonality can never substitute. Such oneness comes with a cost; it takes crucifying the flesh for the sake of love to forge true spiritual unity, whether vertically or horizontally. The real question is, how much are you willing to pay the cost?

The mystery of the marriage has been unfolding since the creation of man. Who would have thought that human history was to be an epic about a Father sending a Servant to seek out a Bride for His Son[50]? Who would have thought that, as Adam marvelled at the first sight of Eve, saying, *"This at last is bone of my bones and flesh of my flesh"*[51], men would one day become His flesh and His bones[52]?

This is a love story written with the golden ink of self-sacrifice; this is a love song that reverberates in the eternal chambers of the heart of God, rising to a crescendo at the revealing of the Last Eve, adorned with the fullness of the glory of God, beautiful as the moon, bright as the sun[53].

(to be continued...)

27. (Pet 1:24) 28. (Rom 12:2) 29. (Luk 11:23) 30. (Php 1:15-18; Mat 23:1-3) 31. (1Co 3:12-15) 32. (Joh 15:16) 33. (Mar 7:9-13; Luk 18:20) 34. (Luk 22:33-34,55-62) 35. (2Ki 6:26-30; Deu 28:52-57) 36. (Eusebius of Caesarea (263-339AD). *The History of the Church*. (1989). Publisher: Penguin Classics. ISBN 9780140445350) 37. (Rom 3:23) 38. (Joh 2:23-24) 39. (Psa 139:15-16; Jer 29:11) 40. (1Co 13:12) 41. (Rom 8:28, NASB) 42. (Psa 139:6) 43. (2Co 12:14) 44. (1Co 13:5,7, NASB) 45. (1Co 9:19-23) 46. (Php 2:6-8) 47. (Mat 10:21; 24:10) 48. (Joh 15:12-13; 1Jn 3:16) 49. (Mat 7:22-23) 50. (Gen 24) 51. (Gen 2:23) 52. (Eph 5:30, NKJV) 53. (Isa 61:10; Psa 45:13-15; Rev 21:2,9-11; Son 6:10)

Printed in Great Britain
by Amazon

46663865R00079